Straight
Talk
for Guys

**Other Books for Teens by Bill Sanders**

*Life, Sex, and Everything in Between*
*Outtakes: Devotions for Girls*
*Outtakes: Devotions for Guys*
*Goalposts: Devotions for Girls*
*Goalposts: Devotions for Guys*
*Tough Turf: A Teen Survival Manual*
*Stand Tall: Learning How to Really Love Yourself*
*Stand Up: Making Peer Pressure Work for You*
*Stand Out: How You Can Become a Strong Leader*
*Almost Everything Teens Want Parents to Know*

# Straight
# Talk
# for Guys

## BILL SANDERS

Fleming H. Revell
A Division of Baker Book House Co
Grand Rapids, Michigan 49516

© 1995 by Bill Sanders

Published by Fleming H. Revell
a division of Baker Book House Company
P.O. Box 6287, Grand Rapids, MI 49516-6287

Printed in the United States of America

### Library of Congress Cataloging-in-Publication Data

Sanders, Bill, 1951–
    Straight talk for guys / Bill Sanders.
        p.    cm.
    ISBN 0-8007-5578-2 (pbk.)
    1. Teenage boys—Religious life. 2. Teenage boys—Conduct of life.
    3. Christian life—Juvenile literature. I. Title.
BV4541.2.S26    1995
248.8'32—dc20                        95-31724

Unless otherwise marked, Scripture quotations are from the New American Standard Bible, © the Lockman Foundation 1960, 1962, 1963, 1968, 1971, 1972, 1973, 1975, 1977.

Scripture quotations marked NIV are from the HOLY BIBLE, NEW INTER-NATIONAL VERSION®. NIV®. Copyright © 1973, 1978, 1984 by International Bible Society. Used by permission of Zondervan Publishing House. All rights reserved.

Scripture quotations marked TLB are from *The Living Bible,* copyright © 1971 by Tyndale House Publishers, Wheaton, Illinois. Used by permission.

# Contents

# Introduction

Join me on an adventure into the mind, heart, and soul. In these pages we'll start a voyage to discover who the awesome Creator really is and meet with the One who is our heavenly Father and wants to be our guide.

This will also be an expedition of trust. You see, I'm on this trip too, and in the process I'm learning to totally lean on God. Though I'm not there yet, I've only a lifetime to go. I don't understand God fully, but I still trust and love him and can honestly say that everything good that has ever come into my life has come from him.

Becoming part of this expedition requires the honesty that goes hand in hand with trust. Like me, you may find that being straight with God isn't nearly as hard as being honest with yourself. In keeping with that honesty, in this book I've sometimes clearly revealed my own lack of faith—including the questions I hardly know how to ask and the answers I have yet to find. I want to respect you by showing you the whole range of faith—including the unanswered questions.

Maybe this book will raise a lot of questions in your life—and maybe we won't find all the answers. But if that leads you to fall in love with our one, true God with every fiber of your being, to trust him when you don't understand, and to count on him to come through for you, I will have achieved my greatest aim.

Living the way God directs us is better by far—even on its worst days—than going the way of the world. Though my words may fail at times, I want you to understand how much your heavenly Father wants to be with you all the way—for the rest of your life.

# 1
# Too Much Freedom?

Why do so few people choose to follow Christ, to be really sold out to the gospel?

It's not as if there weren't enough Bibles, churches, or telecasts that focus on Jesus. It's not as if we never had the chance to tell others or learn about God, either. With all our freedoms—of religion, expression, and speech—Americans have every opportunity to read the Bible, worship God, and express their faith. So why don't we?

I believe that it's a strategy especially designed by Satan.

Imagine that the devil held a town meeting in hell. All the evil spirits took part in designing a scheme that could keep America from Christ.

"Let's burn the Bible," suggests one spirit. "When each one comes off the press, we can supernaturally destroy it. Without the Word, they'll never be able to worship God!"

"No, I don't think we'll need to do that," Satan replies.

"Let's go back to persecuting the church, the way we used to," another demon proposes. "If someone professes Christ, let's make certain people hate him and burn him at the stake. We can tempt them to set fire to Christians' houses and businesses too."

"That happened in Russia and Germany," Satan replies. "Look where it led. People there hunger for God's Word. All over the world, nations send missionaries to Russia. The people of that country are begging Christians to come to their schools. Communism has failed there. The people have seen through our plan to destroy their country."

Several other demons suggest other ways to destroy faith in America, but Satan turns them all down. Finally he stands up. His eyes gleam as he says, "We don't have to do anything, boys. Just sit back and watch. Let the Gideons put Bibles in every hotel room. Let every American family own one, two, three, or even four Bibles. Churches can spring up on every corner.

"Make certain they teach the freedom of religion. Keep Sunday as a day when nobody works and everyone can go to church. We'll make it so easy for them that they'll take it for granted," Satan snarls.

"How do you know it will work?" demand the other demons.

Pride shines out of Satan's eyes as he shouts back from his throne, "Look at what people take for granted the most. In families where Mom and Dad are always there, teens ignore them. Because they've been born with abilities and opportunities, humans make as little of them as possible. They take their eyes for granted; they take their country for granted. Why, even God, who is always there for them, gets ignored.

"Leave God right there," Satan gleefully exclaims. "He stands at the door of their hearts and patiently knocks. Meanwhile, we'll aggressively attack at all times, never taking naps. We'll tempt them with their own lusts, pleasures, and futility.

"All we have to do is leave them free access to God, and they're certain to take him for granted."

Though I'm not seriously suggesting that such a scene took place in hell, I'm certain we do take God for granted. We're complacent and lackadaisical about our faith. Many people expect to have the opportunity of the thief on the cross in the moments before they die.

Some people do get a last chance—my dad was such a man. A year before he died, he was in the hospital. Believing he was on his deathbed, my dad allowed my friend Pastor Will Davis to lead him to the Lord. Just like the thief on the cross, my dad stole eternity. A short time before he expected to face an eternal reward, he trusted Christ. I'm glad for that.

But no one can count on receiving Christ at the last moment. You never know that you'll have my dad's opportunity. Remember, you don't know when you might die in a car wreck, contract a fatal disease that will snatch your life away, or be on the receiving end of an angry teenager's bullet.

Don't live your own way, satisfying the devil, on the off chance that you can repent at the last moment. Don't waste your life when you could reach out and grab Jesus. God has said, "'At the acceptable time I listened to you, and on the day of salvation I helped you'; behold, now is 'the acceptable time,' behold, now is 'the day of salvation'" (2 Cor. 6:2).

Make your choice—and make it now!

# 2
# What's the Difference?

"Christians are no different from the rest of the world. Their divorce rate is nearly as high, they become alcoholics, and they abuse their kids," a friend commented over breakfast recently. I felt shocked and angry at his words, but all the way home from the restaurant I thought about it and decided he was right—absolutely right.

Christian teens write me as frequently as non-Christians. Many seem to be as lost as those who don't know Jesus. If they break up with a boyfriend or girlfriend, they think their lives are ruined. They have sex, drink, party, disrespect their parents, have to be dragged to church, and cheat on tests as much as those who couldn't care less about their relationship with God.

Every day I hear kids from Christian schools complain about their hypocritical parents—just like all the rest of the kids. So what is the problem? Who's at fault? Why are those of us who say we love Jesus no different from the rest of the world?

Don't get me wrong! I'm not trying to judge the rest of the world and leave myself out of it. Quite often I wonder why I don't have more peace in my heart than those with whom I counsel. Why do I get just as angry as the next dad when my kids spill the milk? I can't cover my wrongs with the cute bumper-sticker phrase "Christians are just sinners who have been forgiven." It's more serious than that.

Sure, we can claim we have been saved, because we prayed the prayer at youth group, but believing in Jesus is more than that. Every day, in everything we do, we have to live out the commitment we made. If we want to follow Jesus, we can't take it lightly. It wasn't merely his love that saved us. It was his total suffering and the blood that dripped from his head, side, and back while he hung on the cross for us. The cross has to become more than simply a piece of pretty jewelry—we need to recognize that it was an instrument of death and that Jesus died for the wrongs we've done against God.

Maybe you already know that God loves you. You've heard a thousand sermons on John 3:16, and that verse trips so glibly off your tongue that it doesn't mean much anymore. Many people concentrate on God's love, his shed blood, and the way Christians are supposed to live about as much as they think of the dead fly on the windowsill. Certainly they don't ponder the idea of being salt and light in a lost world. If they hear it in a sermon, by Sunday afternoon they've forgotten about it. Certainly they don't make a daily time for prayer and Scripture reading.

"Yeah," you may respond, "intercessory prayer and a daily quiet time are fine if you are a monk or a pastor, but who has time for them in a tough world where only the strong survive?"

It's because the world can be so tough that you need to spend time in prayer! God's strength and wisdom are what you need when life gets tough.

Living out your faith isn't optional, no matter what your friends or family say. Jesus laid it flat out when he said, "If you love Me, you will keep My commandments" (John 14:15). What could be plainer than that? If you love him, you do what he says. If you aren't keeping the commandments with any regularity, you aren't loving God.

I'm not saying you cannot have an occasional sin that stabs your conscience. If that happens, repent before God and get right with him. But if you are sinning as a way of life, and you don't feel that you are hurting God or your walk with him, you need to rethink why you call yourself a Christian.

**God's strength and wisdom
are what you need
when life gets tough.**

"But doesn't God forgive us, even when we keep on sinning?" you may ask.

God says you show who you really are by the way you act. If you are a Christian, you may make mistakes, but you won't keep acting like an unbeliever. If you are an unbeliever, you won't have a walk with God.

Playing the I'm-saved-because-I-prayed-the-prayer-at-youth-group game will not give you the right to spend eternity with Jesus. Faith means more than what you pray one night; it's a lifestyle decision.

Jesus pulls no punches when he talks about a person's true, deep-down, under-the-skin character. Even though we don't want to hear it, he tells us straight:

Enter by the narrow gate; for the gate is wide, and the way is broad that leads to destruction, and many are those who enter by it. For the gate is small, and the way is narrow that leads to life, and few are those who find it. Beware of the false prophets, who come to you in sheep's clothing, but inwardly are ravenous wolves. You will know them by their fruits. Grapes are not gathered from thorn bushes, nor figs from thistles, are they? Even so, every good tree bears good fruit; but the bad tree bears bad fruit. A good tree cannot produce bad fruit, nor can a bad tree produce good fruit. Every tree that does not bear good fruit is cut down and thrown into the fire. So then, you will know them by their fruits. Not everyone who says to Me, "Lord, Lord," will enter the kingdom of heaven; but he who does the will of My Father who is in heaven. Many will say to Me on that day, "Lord, Lord, did we not prophesy in Your name, and in Your name cast out demons, and in Your name perform many miracles?" And then I will declare to them, "I never knew you; depart from Me, you who practice lawlessness."

Matthew 7:13–23

If you call yourself a Christian, live like one. You should stand out in a crowd for the things you believe, say, and do. That's why you can't live with one foot in sin and the other in heaven. Like oil and water, God and sin don't mix—and they never will.

# 3

# Dittohead

People who agree with the stand of conservative talk-show host Rush Limbaugh call in and say "ditto" or "megaditto." That means they agree with him and appreciate his views on politics and life. They stand with him against abortion and agree that abstinence is the only way to be 100 percent sure you won't get pregnant or contract AIDS. They believe that there is a God and that America needs to return to its moral and spiritual foundations.

Many liberal journalists call these people "dittoheads" and say they can't think for themselves. They claim these "mind-numb" followers could be led by Rush anywhere, at any time, into anything.

Reporters aren't the only ones to toss around such accusations, and Rush Limbaugh's listeners aren't the only ones being denounced. Lots of others accuse Christians of being head-in-the-sand types who are so weak that they can't think for themselves and need a leader.

Maybe these critics haven't figured out that we already do have a leader—Jesus. "You shall follow the LORD your God and fear Him; and you shall keep His commandments, listen to His voice, serve Him, and cling to Him" (Deut. 13:4). I know I've already chosen a leader to follow based on Ephesians 5:1: "Therefore be imitators of God, as beloved children." Serving Jesus means you follow him by serving others with your life: "If anyone serves Me, let him follow Me; and where I am, there shall My servant also be; if anyone serves Me, the Father will honor him" (John 12:26).

Thinking for yourself the way the critics seem to think you should isn't all it's cracked up to be. For twenty-eight years I did it, and I wouldn't recommend it to anyone. During that time, my only reference points for decisions were my feelings and pleasures. It didn't matter to me if what I did was wrong or if I hurt people. My conscience was numb, and my heart had begun to harden.

When I turned my life over to Jesus, I became a new person with a clean heart. My body had become home to the Holy Spirit. With my tender and fresh conscience, I couldn't sin without feeling terrible inside. Even now, seventeen years later, I remain a new person. Jesus makes me feel fresh and gives me hope each and every day.

After experiencing such a real and life-changing rebirth, is it any wonder I want to follow Jesus instead of myself? I'd rather follow Jesus' command than my own inclinations: "If anyone wishes to come after Me, let him deny himself, and take up his cross, and follow Me" (Matt. 16:24).

When people ask why I believe in Jesus, whom I can't see, I tell them my heart has 20/20 vision. I can clearly see who he is and what he has done for me. He has changed my life. As surely as I know my wife and children, I know I am his and he is mine. Jesus said, "The works that I do in My Father's name, these bear witness of Me" (John 10:25). I've seen that witness in my life.

When people say that by giving my life to Jesus I can no longer think for myself, I know it isn't so. For the first time in my life I don't chase after every fad or fashion or give in to peer pressure. I go to the Bible and see what God wants me to do; I filter everything through his holy ideals before I make a choice.

You see, I'd rather please God than all the skeptics and nonbelievers in the universe. They're mistaken when they think that being a dittohead for Jesus means being a blind follower: "Again therefore Jesus spoke to them, saying, 'I am the light of the world; he who follows Me shall not walk in the darkness, but shall have the light of life'" (John 8:12).

When my Creator leads me, he knows what's ahead. That drives away my fear and worry about my life here on earth as well as any concern about what will happen when I die. I know that I can trust him, just as the sheep trust a shepherd. "When he puts forth all his own, he goes before them, and the sheep follow him because they know his voice. . . . My sheep hear My voice, and I know them, and they follow Me" (John 10:4, 27).

Are you in line with the shepherd, or are you a dittohead for Satan?

# 4

## Read the Book

"Why bother to read a book that was written thousands of years ago? What's the point in reading the Bible every day? It's too out-of-date to help someone living in the twentieth century!"

People may not come out and say it, but I know they often think things like that when I tell them I read the Bible. They wonder what it could offer me—or them. Maybe you've asked yourself some of the same questions.

So why should you read the Bible?

No other book in the world is like this one. When you need answers to life's questions, the Bible will show you what God wants you to do. When you are hurting or wondering how to handle life, reading this instruction guide for life will be the equivalent of counseling with God. Because God's Spirit inspired every word in it, we can trust what the Bible says.

"I have a hard time understanding what the Bible says," you may object. That's because you need God's help to comprehend it. Before you start reading, pray for God to guide you: "Open my eyes that I may see wonderful things in your law. I am a stranger on earth; do not hide your commands from me. My soul is consumed with longing for your laws at all times" (Ps. 119:18–20 NIV). Long to understand God's Word, spend time in it, and you can learn more and more.

God wants you to desire him, not the craziness of the world:

Stop loving this evil world and all that it offers you, for when you love these things you show that you do not really love God; for all these worldly things, these evil desires—the craze for sex, the ambition to buy everything that appeals to you, and the pride that comes from wealth and importance—these are not from God. They are from this evil world itself. And this world is fading away, and these evil, forbidden things will go with it, but whoever keeps doing the will of God will live forever.

1 John 2:15–17 TLB

Understanding God's Word takes effort. It's not like reading a magazine that you will throw away next week. "Work hard so God can say to you, 'Well done.' Be a good workman, one who does not need to be ashamed when God examines your work. Know what his Word says and means" (2 Tim. 2:15 TLB). Digging into his Word, thinking about it, and memorizing it enable us to live in God's way instead of our own. Taking the time to read and study it carefully brings us lifelong benefits.

God promises kings that he will bless them and their nations if they follow his Word:

When he takes the throne of his kingdom, he is to write for himself on a scroll a copy of this law, taken from that of the priests, who are Levites. It is to be with him, and he is to read it all the days of his life so that he may learn to revere the LORD his God and follow carefully all the words of this law and these decrees and not consider himself better than his brothers and turn from the law to the right or to the left. Then he and his descendants will reign a long time over his kingdom in Israel.

Deuteronomy 17:18–20

Whether or not you have power over a country, you need wisdom to live the best life you can. Why not tap into God's knowledge by delving into his Word?

What happens when you read something in God's Word and don't like it? Do you have the right to mentally erase it from Scripture? Can you add some good ideas that you don't find there?

No, God's Word is not something you can manipulate:

> And I solemnly declare to everyone who reads this book: If anyone adds anything to what is written here, God shall add to him the plagues described in this book. And if anyone subtracts any part of these prophecies, God shall take away his share in the Tree of Life, and in the Holy City just described.
>
> Revelation 22:18–19 TLB

Take God's Word for what it is—his Spirit-inspired guide for your life—and it will become your greatest resource. I know that's true because seventeen years of Bible reading have shown it to me. When I feel depressed, I find comfort in God's Word. He fills me with worth and purpose as his words flow through my mind and heart.

Try it in your own life, and you'll be able to say the same thing!

# 5

# God or the Big Bang?

If you want to be politically correct, believe in anything *except* a God who has created the universe and every living thing. Many so-called intelligent people have trusted totally in evolution, Darwin, and the Big Bang Theory. As a result, they have left their Creator totally out of the picture.

"Why do you believe God created the world and all of us?" people often ask. I simply answer that he said it, and he never lies. I've thought a lot about who I am and about the One in whom I've put my total trust, life, family, hopes, and dreams.

"But you've never seen him," object the skeptics.

"You are right," I answer. "But I have seen what he has done in my life. He changed me from a totally egotistic, self-serving, not-caring-whom-I-hurt maniac into a child of God. I'm a sinner saved by his grace and love."

Show your Mother-Earth-is-everything, evolution-believing friends God's testimony in the book of Genesis about how the earth came to be. Here are just a few verses from the first chapter:

In the beginning God created the heavens and the earth.
. . . Then God said, "Let the earth sprout vegetation, plants

yielding seed, and fruit trees bearing fruit after their kind, with seed in them, on the earth"; and it was so. . . . And God created the great sea monsters, and every living creature that moves, with which the waters swarmed after their kind, and every winged bird after its kind; and God saw that it was good. . . . And God made the beasts of the earth after their kind, and the cattle after their kind, and everything that creeps on the ground after its kind; and God saw that it was good. . . . And God created man in His own image, in the image of God He created him; male and female He created them. . . . And God saw all that He had made, and behold, it was very good. And there was evening and there was morning, the sixth day.

Genesis 1:1, 11, 21, 25, 27, 31

In case there are any questions, listen to the New Testament testimonies on God's creation:

In the beginning was the Word, and the Word was with God, and the Word was God. He was in the beginning with God. All things came into being by Him, and apart from Him nothing came into being that has come into being.

John 1:1–3

The God who made the world and all things in it, since He is Lord of heaven and earth, does not dwell in temples made with hands.

Acts 17:24

Yet for us there is but one God, the Father, from whom are all things, and we exist for Him, and one Lord, Jesus Christ, by whom are all things, and we exist through Him.

1 Corinthians 8:6

And to bring to light what is the administration of the mystery which for ages has been hidden in God, who created all things.

Ephesians 3:9

And He is the image of the invisible God, the first-born of all creation.

Colossians 1:15

"But I don't believe what I can't see," your friends may object. Explain to them that you *can* see—all it takes is faith: "By faith we understand that the worlds were prepared by the word of God, so that what is seen was not made out of things which are visible" (Heb. 11:3).

All the way to the last book of his wonderful, error-free Bible, God is revealed as the Creator of all things. "Worthy art Thou, our Lord and our God, to receive glory and honor and power; for Thou didst create all things, and because of Thy will they existed, and were created" (Rev. 4:11).

He said it, I believe it, and that settles it for me. Get to know him better, and it can be settled for you too.

# 6

# Cop Scare!

A police car appears in your rearview mirror, and how do you react? If you're like most people, you're scared half out of your wits.

"What have I done wrong?" you wonder as the police car nears you. "Does he know something about me that I don't know? Oh my goodness, I bet I'm speeding." You look at your speedometer, and if it doesn't show the number on the speed-limit sign, you hit your brakes, alerting the policeman to the fact that you were doing something wrong. Your heart beats faster, beads of perspiration form on your forehead, and you start to get really close to God.

"Get me out of this, Lord," you pray. "Help me through this one, and I'll never do it again. I'll never be bad for the rest of my life!"

On those rare occasions when you notice that the speedometer is right on target, you breathe a sigh of relief and are very careful not to do anything wrong while the policeman is behind you. Slow and easy does it. You put on your turn signal a half mile before the turn. You come to a complete stop at the stop sign and stay there for a full minute before moving on so that he can tell you stopped dead.

The other day I found out that being guilt free is wonderful. I'd been hitting some practice golf shots at my favorite little field. The whole time I had a quiet time, just me, my clubs, and the Lord. (I even hit some straight shots, so you know I was feeling good.)

As I drove home, I turned the corner, and a cop pulled up just in back of me. For the first time in a long while, I didn't even feel nervous. I had nothing to hurry for, and peace filled my heart. Even before I looked at my speedometer, I knew I wasn't speeding.

Most of the time when I see a policeman, I have reason to be nervous. I'm in a hurry because I started too late and have to catch up to the clock. Guilt covers me because I know I am in the wrong.

It's the same in my spiritual life. When I don't prepare myself in the morning by giving the day over to the Lord, it seems like an uphill battle all day. You know the feeling: No matter how hard you try or how fast you go, you're always a step behind where you want to be.

Turn every day over to God. Before you go to school, to the game, or to the mall, talk to him. Commit your day to him and tell him you don't want to take any hits that day. Tell him you don't want to do anything that would make him unhappy, because those things linger in your life far too long.

Be pleasing in God's sight, and you will have nothing to worry about. You'll never have to sweat over anything, because you will be guilt free. You will be able to stand in his presence with nothing to hide, no shame to wipe away, no fear to conceal. "The steadfast of mind Thou wilt keep in perfect peace, because he trusts in Thee" (Isa. 26:3). Keep looking to Jesus every day, and you will keep your mind on him.

It's kind of like traveling in front of a cop and not being worried.

# 7

# Could I Do That?

During the last two hours of the movie *Jesus of Nazareth*, Jesus foretold his fate, and the disciples didn't catch the message. Still, it didn't seem to bother him. As he was being mocked and insulted, he merely looked beyond anger, getting even, and the need to look good in the eyes of others. He envisioned God's purpose in his life: He was to be mocked, crowned with thorns, nailed to a cross, and was to die an agonizing death for us. He knew that salvation would come in the end with his resurrection.

Jesus had an eternal perspective. He was able to see past the present imperfections to God's perfect plan. When Jesus told Peter that he would deny him, he looked past the disciple's sin and still loved the disciple. Although Pontius Pilate lorded his earthly power over Jesus, the Messiah looked past that earthly ruler toward eternity with God the Father.

Could I follow in Jesus' footsteps? Could I forgive someone before he hurt me? Could I love someone, knowing I had nothing to gain? Could I serve someone without being noticed? Could I be all God wants me to be, only for the excitement of having integrity before God?

On the other hand, can I bear *not* to do what God calls me to do?

Judas, who had lived with Jesus for three years and heard his teachings, took the cowardly way out and ended his own life after betraying his Master. How alone the onetime disciple must have felt—empty of hope, purpose, and faith. I can imagine his feelings because I know how I feel when I have let Jesus down. I want to hide, be alone, and feel awful.

But I know that things don't have to end the way they did for Judas. You see, Peter gives me hope. Even though he denied Jesus, the Master didn't give up on him. Before Peter had sinned, Jesus said to him: "'I have prayed for you, that your faith may not fail; and you, when once you have turned again, strengthen your brothers'" (Luke 22:32).

Jesus knows you and me and loves us as we are, with all our hang-ups and tobacco breath, with all our sins that are secret from the world (but not from him). All our pains and scars will not stop his love, and he will always look past our humanness and open paradise to us if we will let him in. All we have to do is ask, just like the thief on the cross.

I've always wondered why they punished a thief so cruelly as to hang him on a cross. But they did it to Jesus, and all he did was call the religious leaders of his day hypocrites. Worse than that, he took the spotlight off those leaders and put it on himself.

When we talk about God's desire to be first in our lives, my young son says, "Jesus seems selfish." In a way, God *is* selfish. He wants all of us. But, as always, the choice to let him in is ours.

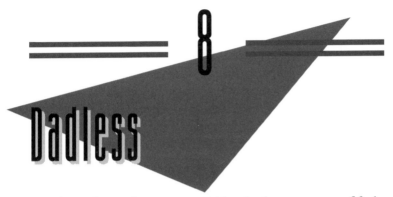

# 8

# Dadless

When I hear of parents and kids who have run out of feelings for each other, it breaks my heart. That's how I felt when I got this letter:

Dear Bill,

I just heard you speak at my school about your dad, how you loved him, and how you miss him since his death.

I used to be real close to my dad. Now we don't talk or even go near each other. I don't care if he sees me graduate from high school or if he never sees me again. He has verbally abused me for so long that I am empty of love for him.

Should I forgive him? How can I do it?

Empty and Hurting

This teenager could not find it in himself to forgive his dad. But he doesn't need to find it in himself because God is so full of love and forgiveness that you don't need any of your own. Empty and Hurting just has to take God's forgiveness and let his love heal his heart.

This teen's dad probably has so much pain hidden deep inside him that he doesn't know how to love his child. Why does he destroy relationships? That dad probably doesn't even know. He might want to love his son but be unable to do so. He may want to build others up instead of tearing them down, but he can't or won't.

Empty and Hurting needs to grow close to God and take care of himself. He should pray for his dad, that he would heal and soften up. Jesus advises us: "But I say to you, love your enemies, and pray for those who persecute you" (Matt. 5:44).

If you have a broken relationship with your parents, God can give you a glorious gift—that gift is the ability to forgive. If you need to forgive your parents, realize that you do it as much for yourself as you do for them. You relieve your own inner pain by dropping that burden. Probably the change won't happen overnight, but as you stay close to Christ, he will free you from the agony you feel today. Jesus said, "Bless those who curse you, pray for those who mistreat you" (Luke 6:28). Though it may be hard to imagine today, he can bring you to the place where you can do it.

> **If you have a broken relationship with your parents, God can give you a glorious gift—that gift is the ability to forgive.**

Peter had someone who persistently sinned against him. So he went to Jesus, to ask him what to do: "Then Peter came and said to Him, 'Lord, how often shall my brother sin against me and I forgive him? Up to seven times?' Jesus said to him, 'I do not say to you, up to seven times, but up to seventy times seven'" (Matt. 18:21–22).

Today Jesus is telling you to forgive. He will not leave you alone in your pain, but he will help bring good out of your situation. He can help you forgive your dad if you will allow him to fill your heart.

Though Joseph was mistreated and even sold into slavery by his brothers, God used it for good. Read the end of his story:

> When Joseph's brothers saw that their father was dead, they said, "What if Joseph should bear a grudge against us and pay us back in full for all the wrong which we did to him!" So they sent a message to Joseph, saying, "Your father charged before he died, saying, 'Thus you shall say to Joseph, "Please forgive, I beg you, the transgression of your brothers and their sin, for they did you wrong."' And now, please forgive the transgression of the servants of the God of your father." And Joseph wept when they spoke to him.
>
> Then his brothers also came and fell down before him and said, "Behold, we are your servants." But Joseph said to them, "Do not be afraid, for am I in God's place? And as for you, you meant evil against me, but God meant it for good in order to bring about this present result, to preserve many people alive. So therefore, do not be afraid; I will provide for you and your little ones." So he comforted them and spoke kindly to them.
>
> Genesis 50:15–21

God wants to comfort you and provide you with a heart full of hope. Cling to your God as you wish you could to your earthly father, and the healing will begin.

# 9

# Do I Really Know God?

"I told a friend that I know God," Bob shared. "And he answered, 'Even the devil knows and believes God is real.' If a person truly knows God, how will he be different from the world?"

"Bob, that's a wise question," I answered. "You should be proud of the maturity that caused you to ask it."

In answer to Bob's question, I've identified seven qualities that set Christians apart from the world—qualities I hope you can see growing in your life:

1. *Christians want to live for God.* These are the people who obey God and follow in his footsteps.

> And by this we know that we have come to know Him, if we keep His commandments. The one who says, "I have come to know Him," and does not keep His commandments, is a liar, and the truth is not in him; but whoever keeps His word, in him the love of God has truly been perfected. By this we know that we are in Him: the one who says he abides in Him ought himself to walk in the same manner as He walked.
>
> 1 John 2:3–6

2. *Christians stand up for God and his truth.* When people try to make them deny God, they stand fast. Read about the power God gave Stephen when he took a stand.

And Stephen, full of grace and power, was performing great wonders and signs among the people. But some men from what was called the Synagogue of the Freedmen . . . rose up and argued with Stephen. And yet they were unable to cope with the wisdom and the Spirit with which he was speaking.

Acts 6:8–10

3. *Christians understand that knowing God is greater than life itself.* No matter what they have to give up, they stand firm with Christ.

What is more, I count all things to be loss in view of the surpassing value of knowing Christ Jesus my Lord, for whom I have suffered the loss of all things, and count them but rubbish in order that I may gain Christ, and may be found in Him, not having a righteousness of my own derived from the Law, but that which is through faith in Christ, the righteousness which comes from God on the basis of faith, that I may know Him, and the power of His resurrection and the fellowship of His suffering, being conformed to His death.

Philippians 3:8–10

4. *Christians want to know more about God.* They study their Bibles and pray regularly. And they allow God's Spirit to work in their lives to make them more like him.

Now for this very reason also, applying all diligence, in your faith supply moral excellence, and in your moral excellence, knowledge; and in your knowledge, self-control, and in your self-control, perseverance, and in your perseverance, godliness; and in your godliness, brotherly kindness, and in your brotherly kindness, love. For if these qualities are yours and are increasing, they render you neither useless nor unfruitful in the true knowledge of our Lord Jesus Christ.

2 Peter 1:5–8

5. *Christians show God's love to others.* Because God loves, his people do too.

Beloved, let us love one another, for love is from God; and everyone who loves is born of God and knows God. The one who does not love does not know God, for God is love. By this the love of God was manifested in us, that God has sent His only begotten Son into the world so that we might live through Him. In this is love, not that we loved God, but that He loved us and sent His Son to be the propitiation for our sins. Beloved, if God so loved us, we also ought to love one another. No one has beheld God at any time; if we love one another, God abides in us, and His love is perfected in us.

1 John 4:7–12

6. *Christians realize they don't know all there is to know about God.* They continually learn more about God, not only to benefit themselves, but to benefit others. "So also you, since you are zealous of spiritual gifts, seek to abound for the edification of the church" (1 Cor. 14:12).

7. *Christians totally trust God for their lives.* Knowing that God will always remain faithful to them, they don't put their trust in other people or in things. "And those who know Thy name will put their trust in Thee; For Thou, O LORD, hast not forsaken those who seek Thee" (Ps. 9:10).

Do these characteristics fit you? If so, you are different from the world around you. Becoming more like God every day is a beautiful thing. Never settle for anything less.

# 10
# Fallen from Heaven

Many people sincerely believe that the only devil in this world is in people like Dennis the Menace. And they are sincerely wrong!

People who don't believe that Satan exists play games with the occult. They see nothing wrong with using Ouija boards or tarot cards to attempt to find out what the future holds. They must not know that the Church of Satan exists or that its members practice witchcraft under the leadership of warlocks.

Satan is alive and well, and you won't recognize him, because he's not wearing a red suit with horns and a tail. No, this onetime wonderful angel separated himself from God and wants to destroy you, if you will let him.

Under the name king of Tyre, Ezekiel 28:12–15 describes the fall of this cherub, who was one of the closest angels to God:

Son of man, take up a lamentation over the king of Tyre, and say to him, "Thus says the Lord GOD,
    'You had the seal of perfection,
    Full of wisdom and perfect in beauty.
    You were in Eden, the garden of God;
    Every precious stone was your covering:
    The ruby, the topaz and the diamond;
    The beryl, the onyx, and the jasper;

The lapis lazuli, the turquoise, and the emerald;
And the gold, the workmanship of your settings
    and sockets,
Was in you.
On the day that you were created
They were prepared.
You were the anointed cherub who covers,
And I placed you there.
You were on the holy mountain of God;
You walked in the midst of the stones of fire.
You were blameless in your ways
From the day you were created,
Until unrighteousness was found in you.'"

Satan separated himself from God by wanting to be god.

How you have fallen from heaven,
O star of the morning, son of the dawn!
You have been cut down to the earth,
You who have weakened the nations!
But you said in your heart,
"I will ascend to heaven;
I will raise my throne above the stars of God,
And I will sit on the mount of assembly
In the recesses of the north.
I will ascend above the heights of the clouds;
I will make myself like the Most High."
Nevertheless you will be thrust down to Sheol,
To the recesses of the pit.

Isaiah 14:12–15

As proof of his own divinity, Jesus said, "I was watching Satan fall from heaven like lightning" (Luke 10:18).

It might have been bad enough if Satan had fallen from heaven on his own, but he brought along others into his sin. All heaven waged war: "And there was war in heaven, Michael and his angels waging war with the dragon [Satan]. And the dragon and his angels waged war" (Rev. 12:7).

The war between Satan and God has not ended; only the turf has changed. Satan deceives and lies, just as he did in the Garden of Eden when he destroyed Adam and Eve. Don't give him a toehold in your life. Instead stay close to the Holy Spirit, and don't begin to play games with God's enemy!

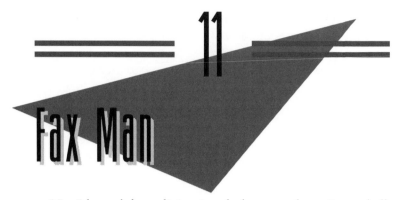

# Fax Man

No, I haven't been living in a hole somewhere. I travel all over the world speaking to people, I write books, and I've been on television and radio. But it was only recently that I got around to buying a fax machine.

It's not as if I didn't know they existed. For the last three years I've been running to the printer to pick up faxes when someone needed to send me something quickly. It's more as if I thought, "These machines will go away if I ignore them long enough."

I finally gave in when a woman wanted me to fax her some materials.

"I'll send them by mail, if that's okay," I suggested.

"We don't use the postal service," she barked and hung up the phone.

Now that was rude, but it showed me that I needed to get a fax machine. Communications today have to be as fast as a McDonald's meal!

So I bought a fax machine, but those things are still totally foreign to me. In fact, it's been a week since it was hooked up, and I'm still scared to death to send one of these babies. Only imagine what I'll do if I receive one! I know there's a manual, but that's what you call "last resort material."

Tim Stewart came to my rescue. He installed my fax machine, programmed it, and showed me how to run it, all for no charge.

But the thing that most impressed me was that not once did he chuckle, laugh, or imply, "You dummy, you don't know how to use a fax machine?" Instead, he treated me like the boss, as if I were paying him. That made me feel really important.

Tim showed me that even an expert in an area should treat people as if they are special, despite the fact that they don't share that expertise.

Is your sport basketball? Do you feel that everyone should be good at it? Do you make fun of others who can't sink a jump shot? Are you a computer whiz? Do you chuckle at anyone who can't do more than turn on the machine? Then you, too, can learn from Tim's example.

My oldest daughter, Emily, isn't really sports minded, but she's willing to try volleyball this year at her new school. Why? Because Arla, the volleyball coach, has given her hope. Arla described a girl who took all year to be able to serve the ball over the net. During the game when her serve went over, the whole team cheered and the house came down.

Arla has gently given my daughter hope about trying something new and courage to venture out into a different area. An accepting attitude on the coach's part helps Emily strive for new heights.

Jesus was the ultimate gentle teacher. One day his disciples were arguing over which one was the greatest. Instead of blowing his top, he taught them with respect:

> And an argument arose among them as to which of them might be the greatest. But Jesus, knowing what they were thinking in their heart, took a child and stood him by His side, and said to them, "Whoever receives this child in My name receives Me; and whoever receives Me receives Him who sent Me; for he who is least among you, this is the one who is great."
>
> Luke 9:46–48

Tim and Arla have helped me assess myself. Do I act humbly if I have to give people advice on writing a book or giving a speech? I hope I won't be cocky and self-important if they do ask for advice. After all, everyone has his or her specialty—and I still don't know much about fax machines!

So the next time someone admits that he hasn't seen the latest movie, don't scoff. If a friend hasn't heard of your brand-name clothes, don't pick on her. Things aren't important—people are.

Be gentle with people—just like Jesus.

# 12

## He Fixed Me!

"Have you asked Jesus to forgive you for your sins?" the counselor asked a little boy she had seen wandering Cessna Stadium in Wichita, Kansas, searching for someone to talk to. Tears in his eyes, he assured her he had.

"Do you know what that means?" she asked.

With a child's innocence and beauty, he answered, "Yes, he fixed me!"

Nearly fifteen thousand teens had shown up to hear Rich Mullins and his Ragamuffin Band play and listen to the preaching of Joseph Jennings. The boy was one of those who responded to the call to take Jesus' words seriously: "If you confess with your mouth Jesus as Lord, and believe in your heart that God raised Him from the dead, you shall be saved."

Despite efforts of the ACLU to shut down the meeting and a newspaper boycott of the event, the crowds kept coming to hear our "dangerous" message of hope and love. Those of us who had prayed and worked so hard to put together this event saw our dreams come true as gang members turned their lives over to Jesus, some crying out, "I'm tired of shooting and hurting people. Help me, God." Others cried tears of joy as they repented of their sins. God had his way in broken lives, making them whole and clean.

So much wisdom lay in the little boy's words. Most of us don't even realize we need anything, let alone fixing! By saying that, he showed the world that not everything was perfect in his life.

"No kidding!" God could say when we tell him we're broken. No one needs to pretend in front of him! He realizes how much each one of us needs forgiveness.

Once we realize that he is the potter and we are the clay, God can do what he does best—fix us! He says, "I love it when my children realize they are broken. I've already told them, 'There is no one who does good, not even one' (Ps. 14:3). And I wasn't kidding when I said, 'There is none righteous, not even one' (Rom. 3:10). To make it even easier to understand, I said, 'For all have sinned and fall short of the glory of God' (Rom. 3:23).

"I described David as a man after my own heart, after he had sinned and needed a fix-it man for his heart and spirit. He understood, 'It is a broken spirit you want—remorse and penitence. A broken and a contrite heart, O God, you will not ignore' (Ps. 51:17 TLB)."

How happy God was to hear one little boy say what all creation should be expressing. Don't we all need to seek the One who can truly fix it all?

# 13

# Flawless before God

If you are saved, is it possible to be sinless before God? Yes and no.

You see, once you accept Christ as your Lord and Savior, you are born again. God gives you eternal life with heaven as your home. He casts your sins in the deepest part of the sea; they are as far from God as the east is from the west. In his sight, we are flawless. "When you were dead in your sins and in the uncircumcision of your sinful nature, God made you alive with Christ. He forgave us all our sins" (Col. 2:13 NIV).

But when it comes to living a sinless life, even though you are saved, it's impossible. Someone who says he lives 100 percent free from sin is lying.

Before they are saved, many people will say, "I'm not a sinner." What they mean is that they've never committed any huge, gigantic, earthshaking sins—nothing on the Ten Most Wanted list of crimes. They've never murdered or abused anybody, robbed a bank, and so on. But God spoke through Isaiah years ago and said, "We all, like sheep, have gone astray, each of us has turned to his own way" (Isa. 53:6 NIV).

But James 4:17 says: "Anyone, then, who knows the good he ought to do and doesn't do it, sins." If you know something is wrong, and you do it anyway, you have sinned. When you know what is *right* and don't do it, that is *also* sin. Our only solution to the problem lies in God. Every day we need to turn our lives over to Christ again. We need to constantly rededicate ourselves to him.

If we don't think we need him, we won't reach out to Jesus. We put him in the position of the father who wanted to save his drowning son, but the boy would not reach for his hand. The father wanted to help but was denied access. In our rebellion, we deny Jesus the opportunity to hold our hands and help us through life.

As we walk through many days of our lives, God throws us a life preserver. Thinking we are perfectly safe on dry ground, we don't grab on. If we had fallen out of a raft in the rushing Colorado River, you can bet we'd grab on—we'd be scared to death. We'd grasp that life-sustaining piece of Styrofoam and be thankful for it. But as long as we think we're on solid ground, we'd rather do it our way, thank you.

When we're saved, our sins are forgiven through Christ's death. But that doesn't mean that we don't sin anymore. So when we goof up, we need to pick ourselves up and ask God for strength.

Look at some of the life preservers God uses to make salvation possible:

1. *He gave his life.* "For God so loved the world that he gave his one and only Son, that whoever believes in him shall not perish but have eternal life" (John 3:16 NIV).
2. *God's unfailing love.* "Turn, O LORD, and deliver me; save me because of your unfailing love" (Ps. 6:4 NIV).
3. *God's mercy.* "Keep yourselves in God's love as you wait for the mercy of our Lord Jesus Christ to bring you to eternal life" (Jude 21 NIV).
4. *God's grace.* "For the grace of God that brings salvation has appeared to all men" (Titus 2:11 NIV).

5. *God's free gift.* "For the wages of sin is death, but the gift of God is eternal life in Christ Jesus our Lord" (Rom. 6:23 NIV).

Don't walk around God's life preservers, even if they land on dry ground. Spend your time doing the best you can with God's help. Concentrate more on obeying God than on striving for perfection.

# 14

# Look What I Found!

During our vacation in Fort Myers, Florida, over and over I heard my children say, "Look what I found, Daddy," or, "Wait! Look what I've got!" Every little shell was a prize to them.

Now, many of their "prizes" were smaller pieces of larger shells that any real shell collector would toss aside. And most people who had already picked up ten of the same type of shell would have cast the next one aside—but not my kids. In their eyes, each one was a masterpiece. They planned to take some to their classmates, give some to Grandma, and put others in their rooms.

I carried the plastic bag that held these treasures, and it got pretty heavy with all our finds. When the question became, "Can we keep it, Daddy?" I couldn't break their hearts. "Sure," I answered. Though we almost had to pay an excess-baggage fee on the way back, we got all the treasures home.

To God, our cares and concerns are just like those broken pieces of shells. When our worries and cares are important to us, they are of vital importance to God. He cares—*really* cares. And his bag is big enough for all our problems and hurts. All our tears fit into his love-lined, peace-filled pouch.

When Jesus prayed, "My Father, if it is possible, let this cup pass from Me" (Matt. 26:39), that cup probably included awful things we will never know about. Remember, he descended into hell so that we wouldn't have to. His love is so grand that he willingly suffered at the hands of the executioners and died an agonizing death on the cross.

"Look at this, Jesus." "Listen to this, Father." Go to him with your troubles, because he is a loving, helping Father. When you come to him with cracked, broken parts, he puts them back together again. It's not merely a repair job, either, because he replaces them with a brand-new, beautiful masterpiece.

# 15

## Improve Your Game

"Jesus Christ!" Those words aren't a prayer when a golfer yells them out on the course. A friend and I had teamed up with a couple of other fellows we didn't know, and that's what one of them yelled whenever he had trouble with his game.

Finally I said, "I've got the answer to your golf game."

"What's that?" he asked disgustedly.

"You'd do better at this sport if you talked to him before the shot, rather than waiting until after."

For the rest of the day, that man didn't use profanity! I spent four more hours with him, and he didn't take the Lord's name in vain the whole time.

As we walked up the eighteenth fairway, this man stopped, looked me in the eye, and asked, "Why was it so important to you that I not swear like that?"

I had the chance to tell him that Jesus brought my wife and me back together when our marriage was about to split apart. I told him that Jesus loved us so much that he died on the cross for us. "On Christmas day 1978, when Jesus took me into his arms and I gave my life to him, I was assured of salvation. Since then he has never left me—and never will. He is the reason I live and my purpose for sharing with teens in schools around the country. He is the reason I get up in the morning," I explained.

As he started to walk away, he stopped once more and commented, "You're the first person to challenge my profanity in over five years."

Wow! Look what a little conviction and courage did.

The next time you feel you need to say something in God's defense, don't let a lack of words stop you. Remember that God told Moses, "Now then go, and I, even I, will be with your mouth, and teach you what you are to say" (Exod. 4:12). God just wanted Moses to be willing to let God speak through him.

God is looking for people who are brave enough to stand up for him. If you do that, I believe God will shower down blessings on you. Many of us are too ashamed to stand up for God when someone takes his name in vain. But you'd stand up for your mom if someone meant her harm. If someone ridiculed your team, you'd have words to say. When a buddy of yours gets cut down, you jump right in.

**God is looking for people who are brave enough to stand up for him.**

I think God is more important than our team. He's a mom and dad and hope giver all wrapped up in one. So make a stand for him. And maybe someday a person you've spoken to will meet you on the green and say, "Thanks, you've made a difference in my life."

# 16

# Seeking God's Grace

Recently my friend Jim's mother died. Jim had been very close to his mother and felt a deep grief. Because he is a pastor, his brothers and sisters asked him to speak at the funeral. Though pain overwhelmed him and he doubted that he was up to the challenge, Jim told his family he would pray about it.

While he was praying, God gave Jim a clear, inner conviction that he was the man for the job. Before he chose to act, Jim didn't know if he was physically and emotionally able to speak at his mother's funeral. But once he decided to follow God's leading, God gave him the grace and the strength to act on it.

The steps Jim took are a good formula that will ensure success in your projects, too. Before you start anything, pray about it. Get the conviction in your heart and decide you can accomplish it.

Now, obviously, there are many things that you could never accomplish, even if you spent years praying about them. You just might not have the physical abilities to be an Olympic swimmer. Or the gifts, special talents, and deep desire to be a mountain climber might not be part of your makeup.

However, you might be the one who could reach a certain person for Christ, write a book that will help people who are suffering emotionally, or preach the gospel to people who have never heard. Maybe you can take clothes to needy people in another part of your town, be a peacekeeper in your school, or encourage a teacher who is ready to quit.

When you've prayed, God may not announce what you should do by speaking through the clouds in a loud voice. (Though he can speak out loud, he doesn't do it often.) More than likely you will feel a nudge, an urge to do something. At this point, you need to spend time in prayer to find out if it's only your own desire or God's will. God will never tell you to do something that is wrong or that goes against what he's already said in his Word. But if you will listen and seek to do what's right, God can give you a conviction that this is his will.

Finally, you will have to make up your mind to do what God has shown you. Many people fall short at this point. They never say, "With God's help, I am going to try my best to do this."

Andy, a friend of mine from high school, decided to run his own business. Though he had wanted to move out on his own for a long time, he waited to take the plunge. He was held back by fears that he would have to move, that he would need to get out of his comfort zone, and that he'd have to work longer hours, taking him away from his family.

When I talked to Andy, it was obvious to me that God was shedding his grace on this man. He had the strength to reach his goal, and he wanted to serve the Lord in his business. Doubts for his family and fears about losing a regular paycheck kept him from experiencing the grace God had available for him. Once Andy took the step, that grace became apparent.

God's grace is available to us all if we are willing to go after it. But like the Israelites, we have to step into the Jordan River before God will part it in front of us. "And when those who carried the ark came into the Jordan, and the feet of the priests carrying the ark were dipped in the edge of the water, . . . the waters which were flowing down from above stood and rose up in one heap" (Josh. 3:15–16).

God won't force you to go out and do good things for others. But once you commit yourself to him, I believe he will pour out his grace, strength, and blessing as you've never seen it before.

The next time your heart tells you what to do, remember Jim's formula. Pray, to see if it is something you can do. Deep down if you feel it is and yet shyness or worry holds you back, pray some more. Once you feel God's leading, remember that the two of you together can handle anything. After all, God is still in the miracle business.

Then say, "I will." Though the earth may not shake in response to your choice, plod steadily on in your journey. Eventually you will reach your God-given goal.

Every time I speak in a school, I believe I can do it, though there are many who might do it better. Then I determine that I will do it, and God has always given me the grace, strength, and words.

God wants you to reach your goal. Go for it!

# 17

# I Don't Know How This Happened

"I don't know how this happened!" began a man who met with me for an hour to tell me of his troubles. He explained he'd been having an affair with a woman and felt he really loved her. Staying with his family had become harder and harder.

The whole mess began with just a glance here and there and an occasional smile from a coworker. Then it became a note here, a "How are you?" there, a drink after work, and a secret luncheon meeting.

Now his fun and games were about to destroy two families, with six children between them. His selfish desires would leave them without full-time parents. Those youngsters would turn into rubber bands, snapped back and forth—a weekend here, a few days there, vacation here this summer and there next summer.

As a teen, you aren't at risk for infidelity. But you may be at risk for falling into sin without realizing it. Like that man, you may find yourself in a situation and want to cry, "I don't know how it happened!"

"It happened like this," I told the man. "You took the first look, and you liked it. You knew it was wrong, but you chose to take the second look. You felt you were young again, and you liked that. When you met for lunch, your gut told you that you were wrong. If your kids were with you, you wouldn't be there. If your wife had been anywhere nearby, you would have lost your appetite. You obviously didn't think that God was there at all."

I challenge young people and married people to stay pure for sure. For example, I don't go into bars because doing that almost ruined my life. I don't go where I'd be vulnerable with other women because that almost ruined my marriage. Holly is too special to me to take a first or second look at any other woman. So when I go to schools with a lot of women teachers and teenage girls, I make certain I put my testimony up front. I always let people know that I'm sold out to God. While that may cost me a speech now and then, it won't cost me my marriage. My wife is too special for me to sin anymore.

I think of my children, Emily, Crystal, and Brandon. How could I face them? How could I look them in the eye and say, "I don't know how it happened. I just fell in love with this other woman, and now I must leave. We're going to get married and live somewhere else"? I couldn't do that.

All I have to do is spend five minutes thinking about what God saved me from. When I think of the life he's given me and the one he allowed me to leave behind, I feel humbled.

What about you? Do you

- put yourself in a position to commit sexual sin? Going to a secluded spot with your girlfriend will almost always lead to actions where selfishness replaces respect.
- go into tests unprepared and willing to cheat to get a good grade?
- cruise around town with friends who smoke pot and do other drugs? Beware or they will influence you without your realizing it.

- find it easy to gossip about others? If so, one day you may come face to face with someone who's heard you've been talking about him and be greatly embarrassed.

Satan is waiting to destroy each of us. He always uses sneak attacks, and you will be his latest victim if you don't

1. stay in the Word. Read the Bible every day.
2. spend some time alone each day talking to God.
3. memorize Bible verses. Hide them in your mind and heart.
4. become an active part of a Bible preaching church.
5. help others as a way of life.

When you allow yourself to sin, I hope you don't use the excuse "I just don't know how this happened." Because you *do* know how it happened, even if you can't admit it to yourself.

# 18

## Tough Prayer

"It's hard for me to pray," Chad admitted. "I never get anything out of it. Why do some of us have such a tough time spending time with God in prayer? I know I love God. Why should it be so hard?"

If, like Chad, you have difficulties with your quiet time, make certain you are not dousing the power in your prayer life with these eight prayer killers:

1. *Worry.* Have you ever spent a lot of time worrying about your problems and very little time in prayer? Worry gets you nowhere and distances you even more from God. "Be anxious for nothing, but in everything by prayer and supplication with thanksgiving let your requests be made known to God" (Phil. 4:6).

2. *Disobedience.* Straighten out your life instead of going in the opposite direction of God's will. If you don't, you will suffer the reward of the disobedient:

Then they will cry out to the LORD,
But He will not answer them.
Instead, He will hide His face from them at that time,
Because they have practiced evil deeds.

Micah 3:4

If you aren't obeying God or are living a sinful life, you are wasting your time playing religion. Get real and get right with God. Then talk to him every day.

3. *Doubting God's power.* When you do nothing but question God and his willingness to help you, you won't get far. God wants to help you do the right thing, but you have to give him a chance to work in your life.

> But if any of you lacks wisdom, let him ask of God, who gives to all men generously and without reproach, and it will be given to him. But let him ask in faith without any doubting, for the one who doubts is like the surf of the sea driven and tossed by the wind. For let not that man expect that he will receive anything from the Lord, being a double-minded man, unstable in all his ways.
>
> James 1:5–8

Know in your heart that God can do all; then go to him in prayer.

4. *Habitual lack of prayer.* When prayer gets tough, don't give up, because if you do, your prayer life can go entirely down the drain. Not praying can become a deadly habit that kills off your spiritual life. "Moreover, as for me, far be it from me that I should sin against the LORD by ceasing to pray for you; but I will instruct you in the good and right way" (1 Sam. 12:23). Trust God and talk to him often.

If you don't pray, don't be surprised if God doesn't give you many of the things you want: "You do not have because you do not ask" (James 4:2).

Does God seem far from you? Keep on praying. He's right beside you, even if you can't see him.

5. *Being out of fellowship with Jesus.* Just as you have to go to some trouble to keep your other friendships strong, you have to make an effort to stay close to Jesus. Remaining in him means you live within his commands and rules for your life. "If you abide in Me, and My words abide in you, ask whatever you wish, and it shall be done for you" (John 15:7).

6. *Being filled with arrogance and pride.* Come to God with your head in the clouds, full of "me-itis," and God will not listen to you. After all, if you act like you think you're God, why should he listen? He's God, not you. Depending on how you act, you can receive much from God or nothing. "There they cry out, but He does not answer because of the pride of evil men" (Job 35:12). "But He gives a greater grace. Therefore it says, 'God is opposed to the proud, but gives grace to the humble'" (James 4:6).

7. *Hypocrisy.* Don't try to flatter God with words while you are living for the devil. "But they deceived Him with their mouth, and lied to Him with their tongue" (Ps. 78:36). God hates it when we don't walk our talk. Most people don't much care for that kind of attitude either!

8. *Idolatry.* You don't need to park a golden calf in your front yard to be worshiping an idol. Your own popularity, your need to be number one, money, clothes, car, music, or dates can come before God. God says to avoid it: "Therefore, my beloved, flee from idolatry" (1 Cor. 10:14). "Little children, guard yourselves from idols" (1 John 5:21).

Even if you feel as if God is on the other side of the Grand Canyon, he's waiting patiently to hear from you. Eliminate these prayer stoppers from your life, and again the joy of your faith will flow.

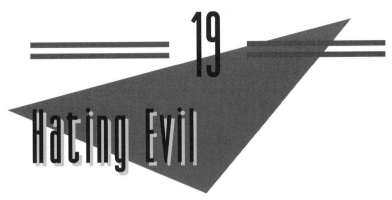

# Hating Evil

I love to get letters like this one:

Dear Bill,
    What does it mean to "hate evil"? If I love Jesus, isn't that enough? I want to be a strong Christian and would appreciate your help.
                                    Searching Christian

Searching Christian is reading his Bible and taking it seriously. He's attempting to do what God commands—or he would never have asked that question.

When it comes to hating evil and fighting back against it, God has not left us helpless. He gives us lots of guidelines:

*Be smart, don't start.* When you love God, you will learn to hate evil. Then you won't even start being involved in sin: "The fear [respect] of the LORD is to hate evil; pride and arrogance and the evil way, and the perverted mouth, I hate" (Prov. 8:13). Hating what God calls evil puts you under his protection: "Hate evil, you who love the LORD, who preserves the souls of His godly ones; He delivers them from the hand of the wicked" (Ps. 97:10).

*Go against your sin nature.* Fighting back against evil doesn't come naturally. We have a bent toward it that comes right from the heart. "The heart is more deceitful than all else" (Jer. 17:9). "Out of the heart come evil thoughts" (Matt. 15:19). "Light is come into the world, and men loved the darkness rather than the light" (John 3:19). "There is none righteous, not even one" (Rom. 3:10).

*You will get caught.* "You Can Run, But You Can't Hide" is the name of this familiar tune. The song is sin, the circulation is all-time best-seller, and the results are always the same: even if you think you get away with wrong, God always knows. "Behold, you have sinned against the LORD, and be sure your sin will find you out" (Num. 32:23).

*Evil will lead to more evil.* When you lust after sin (anything outside the will of God for your life), the payoff is more lust. "Do not be deceived, God is not mocked; for whatever a man sows, this he will also reap. For the one who sows to his own flesh shall from the flesh reap corruption" (Gal. 6:7–8).

*Sin will be the master; you're the slave.* Did you know that we become slaves to sin when we give in to it? I hate the thought of having the Father of Lies, Satan, as my master. For twenty-eight years he was, while I ran from Jesus. I have numerous scars that daily remind me to run from the one who would love to ruin me. "Do you not know that when you present yourselves to someone as slaves for obedience, you are slaves of the one whom you obey, either of sin resulting in death, or of obedience resulting in righteousness?" (Rom. 6:16).

*God grants our requests for pain.* Insist on sinning, and God won't stop you. He will feel brokenhearted and long for you to return to him, but he gave each of us moral wills and the capacity to choose between right and wrong. You can choose wrong.

Don't forget that you also earn the consequences of your choices.

> They quickly forgot His works;
> They did not wait for His counsel,

But craved intensely in the wilderness,
And tempted God in the desert.
So He gave them their request,
But sent a wasting disease among them.

Psalm 106:13–15

"For the wages of sin is death" (Rom. 6:23). "But he who sins against me injures himself; All those who hate me love death" (Prov. 8:36).

I'm praying that you will be wise enough to see sin for what it is, pure enough to want to run from it, humble enough to call to God when temptation is before you, and bold enough to flee when trouble is near. Learn to hate evil, and Satan won't get the best (or worst) of you.

> **Be wise enough to see sin for what it is, pure enough to want to run from it, humble enough to call to God when temptation is before you, and bold enough to flee when trouble is near. Learn to hate evil, and Satan won't get the best (or worst) of you.**

When you are willing to do this, you could be used by God to have an impact on our whole nation. Only God can make us wise and save our nation, but first he needs people willing to:

*Totally give themselves to God.* "Offer your bodies as living sacrifices, holy and pleasing to God. . . . Do not conform any longer to the pattern of this world, but be transformed by the renewing of your mind. Then you will be able to test and approve what God's will is" (Rom. 12:1–2 NIV).

*Stay pure, pray, and produce.* "If you abide in Me, and My words abide in you, ask whatever you wish, and it shall be done for you. By this is My Father glorified, that you bear much fruit, and so prove to be My disciples" (John 15:7–8).

*Let God take over.* "But where sin increased, grace abounded all the more" (Rom. 5:20).

Your world, family, and school desperately need you today as you hate what God hates and follow his commands. Even if they don't realize it, you have the answer they are looking for. Please God instead of following your own desires and pleasures, and you will be so much wiser.

# 20

# Raising Real Characters in a Happy Home

"What you plant is what you get." It's always true. You plant corn, water and fertilize the ground, and unless something destroys your crop, in a few months you have knee-high stalks of corn. No matter how hard you work and hope, if you plant corn you won't get beans.

Family life grows in a similar way. Plant words of loving-kindness, and you'll sprout love and concern. Plant criticism and complaints, and you will grow bitterness and resentment.

There's a right way and a wrong way to build a family. But the good news is that, when you begin your own home, you can have a say in what you grow.

Perhaps you look at your family today and say, "Sure, Mom and Dad weren't perfect, but they've done their best. I appreciate all they've done for me." Or maybe you're more inclined to say, "If I ever have a home and family, it sure won't be like this." Either way, you can build a happy home by understanding what God has in mind for the family. A solid foundation in him is the only basis for a really strong family.

Just as you can tell a tree by its roots, which anchor it during a storm, you can tell a family by the depth of its moral foundation. A stable family's members know right from wrong, and they act out their convictions in their family life by treating each other in the right way. Mom and Dad do not condone underage drinking or sex outside of marriage. They encourage each family member to treat others with respect. In this environment, everyone is built up instead of destroyed.

Another aspect of a stable life is balance. Families remain strong when members combine the mental, physical, spiritual, and social aspects of life in a healthy way. For example, those who focus on social life while avoiding God's call soon find themselves in trouble. But so will those who spend all their time in church and don't set aside time at home with their families.

"Keeping up with the Joneses" by having the latest-model car, biggest house, and largest paycheck usually spells death to family life. When Dad works a lot of overtime, the kids never see him. So it should be no surprise when Johnny and Jane reach their teens and think of their father as a stranger. Their home was built on sinking sand instead of on the firm foundation of a powerful love for God and their parents.

Build your life on the solid rock—Jesus—and you can turn around that kind of family history. Spend time with him in prayer and in his Word to learn what it takes to build relationships with people instead of your stock portfolio. Discover how God wants you to share your life with the people you love most instead of staring into a computer or spending too much time at the factory.

If you see the world through the lenses of the latest fads, you are heading for trouble. Right and wrong become changeable ideas, and you'll bend them to suit your situation.

When Joshua was about to lead the Israelites into the Promised Land, he challenged them with the words, "As for me and my house, we will follow the LORD" (Josh. 24:15). It didn't matter what the latest fad was or who disagreed with him. Joshua had set his family's course—obeying God no matter what.

In making that decision, Joshua showed his family the right way and walked in it. Not even the man with the biggest mouth or the woman with the loudest complaints could deter him from his path. By standing up for God, he became a lesson to his children and the entire nation of Israel.

Having a happy family may not be the easiest goal you ever set for yourself. No one has a perfect family life by a long shot. If you recognize unhealthy patterns in your present family, you will have to work hard to change them. Change is never comfortable. But if you always do what you've always done, you'll always get what you've always gotten. Even in what seems like an absolutely hopeless situation, you can have hope. This difficult change could turn your life around for the better if you let it.

Work together with God to form a happy life by building your own character. Spend time in his Word, make the right decisions, lift up others, and find balance in your life. If your family already understands this, fine; if not, you may be able to show them what it takes to make a better life.

Remember, the family was part of God's plan. He knows how to build it, and in troubled times we can turn to him.

# 21

# The Great Imitator

Amazed, I watched my five-year-old son ride around the neighborhood, waving to each person he passed and yelling, "Your lawn looks great," or, "How are you doing, Mrs. Smith? What a great day!" Then he stopped his bike, put down one foot, draped the other leg over the center bar, leaned on the handle bars, and shot the breeze for a few minutes. Finally he rode home.

"How did he get the courage and develop the confidence to be so outgoing?" I wondered. With a shock, it hit me—he was following my example!

Whether or not I like it, my kids imitate who I am. Though they may not think about it too often, they are influenced by my outlook on life because they're around me every day and watch the way I act. They naturally do what I do.

If it's so natural to follow in our parents' footsteps, why do we have trouble following God's example? After all, isn't he our heavenly Father? Ephesians 5:1 advises us: "Follow God's example in everything you do just as a much loved child imitates his father" (TLB). But do we do that?

It's easy for my kids to know what I'm like because they spend time with me. But if we don't put in any effort to learn God's Word and try to imitate his ways, we will remain strangers from our Creator. Though we may be able to identify which commercial goes with which sitcom, the top hits on MTV, or how many people got murdered in the latest Freddy Krueger movie, we don't know how to be like Jesus.

Maybe your spiritual life is limited to the fact that you can only tell people that Jesus never sinned and that he died and rose again about two thousand years ago. Maybe your friends say the Bible is old-fashioned and most of the stories never really happened. And maybe you'd be embarrassed to death if anyone ever saw you with a Bible.

Now be honest. Does that sound familiar? If so, then you're not following God consistently.

Start following Jesus' example today. Find out about him, get to know him, and spend time with him. Talk to your friends about him, and hang around with those who know him.

If that's tough for you, ask yourself: "Whose style am I imitating—Hollywood's or the Holy One's?" The choice is all yours.

To know God's ways, you don't need to have the entire Bible memorized. Before you do something, simply ask yourself two questions: "Would Jesus do this?" and "Will I be proud of this tomorrow?"

Pretty simple, isn't it? Live that way, and you'll also become an example to others. Paul encouraged others to follow his example as a Christian by writing:

> For although you may have ten thousand others to teach you about Christ, remember that you have only me as your father [meaning spiritual father—the one who led them to Christ]. For I was the one who brought you to Christ when I preached the Gospel to you. So I beg you to follow my example, and do as I do.
>
> 1 Corinthians 4:15–16 TLB

That's an awesome responsibility. Pray with me:

> Dear Lord, help us to love you enough to lead others to you and to live in such a way that we can challenge anyone to follow our example. Amen.

# 22
# Developing Your Inner Passion

"How do you stay motivated talking to teens? For fifteen years you've been doing this. How can you get excited about talking with a thousand junior-high students on a Friday afternoon after a sugary lunch in a ninety-degree gymnasium with a failing sound system where everything bounces off the walls?" I've been asked.

"It's simple," I answer. "The passion inside me is sustained every time I answer another hurting kid's letter. All I have to do is read through a stack of mail to realize that though I have to leave my family and bear the pain of separation, I'm thankful God called me to this task."

You, too, can stay on fire for a cause, if you develop an inner passion that burns brightly in the face of defeat. Something that's very important to you can sustain you when you feel tired and unmotivated and don't want to act. To make your mark for the Lord, you'll need such a passion.

I'll never forget a letter I got from a hurting and confused teen:

Dear Bill,

Two days ago I was ready to give up on life. I had my dad's .22 rifle loaded and hidden under my bed. I planned to use it the next morning before anyone else was awake.

But then my mom came in with your book *Tough Turf* and asked me to read it. I figured I had nothing to lose because in fifteen hours I'd kill myself. So I gave the book a try.

Well, I read the whole book, and I promise you that because of your words I will never attempt suicide again.

Grateful Reader

When I think of the hundreds of similar letters I receive, it spurs me on to develop my best speeches and to give them with as much enthusiasm as I can muster, even on days I feel tired. No matter how unresponsive the audience, or whether I am being paid, I want to do my best for teens who need to hear what God wants me to say.

Part of my desire is a gift from God. Without him, I couldn't continue. How often I get a call from school staff members who aren't sure how my name came to them. Though they don't know where the information originated, they have my number and know they want me to speak. I believe this supernatural method is God's way of showing me that he's in control.

Is something keeping you from developing inner passion? Perhaps you need to stay sin free, but you keep giving in to a weakness. If so, follow these steps:

1. Identify your weak spot.
2. Ask yourself, "What will keep me on God's path when I am tempted to sin?"
3. Write down the answer and hide it in your heart so you won't forget it.

Some teens have a premarital-sex weakness. They can't understand that when they spend time with a certain type of person and go on a certain type of date, they will goof up and have regrets.

Hundreds of teens have shared with me about their weakness for alcohol. Every time they drink, something bad happens. They say words they regret, alienate friends and family, and hurt others or themselves. Despite all this, they can't recognize that alcohol is their enemy. They haven't dealt with it.

To develop an inner passion you have to plan ahead, deciding what you will and will not do. If it's sin, you'll have to decide to turn from it.

Inner passion starts with a decision. "How long will you waver between two opinions?" asked Elijah in 1 Kings 18:21. "If the LORD is God, follow him; but if Baal is God, follow him" (NIV). Baal was an idol of that day, and the Israelites had to choose. So which will you choose—Satan or God?

> God has a purpose for you, but he can't move stationary feet. Shut this book right now and spend time with God. Present him with your unique personality and weaknesses, and ask him to make you strong.

God has great plans for you if you will take his path. I no longer get nervous when I speak before teens, because I know I have a job to do. I've left behind the skinny kid from a small town who was swayed by the crowd and did things that he regrets to this day. I've been called to a purpose, and I will not be turned from that.

God has a purpose for you, but he can't move stationary feet. Shut this book right now and spend time with God. Present him with your unique personality and weaknesses, and ask him to make you strong.

You'll develop that God-given inner passion.

# 23
# Tired of the Killing

Several thousand people had just come down onto the field at Cessna Stadium in Wichita, Kansas. Rich Mullins had sung, Joseph Jennings had preached the loving, saving grace of Jesus, and these people were responding to the invitation to turn their lives over to Christ.

I was helping to get kids into groups where the trained counselors could share what it meant to be sorry for your sins and ask Christ into your heart. Suddenly I heard a counselor cry, "Gang member, gang member. Someone come over here! Gang member."

What was the trouble? Did the gang member have a gun? Drugs? Was someone's life at stake?

I found the counselor with his arm around Tom, a shaking, weeping eighteen-year-old who stood about six foot four and weighed about 240 pounds.

"He needs your help," the counselor stated as I approached.

I looked Tom in the eye, placed my hands on his shoulders, and asked, "Did you just accept Jesus as your Lord and Savior?"

He couldn't respond.

"Are you my new brother in Christ?" I questioned.

He still didn't answer, but the flow of tears increased, and he shook even more.

God pushed me, and my arms went around Tom as God seemed to say, "Show him my love."

He grabbed on to me, nearly crushing my back. Still sobbing, he said in my ear, "I'm tired of the killing, tired of the shooting, tired of the pain. Help me. Help me."

Tom sat down with me. Tired of the pain he inflicted upon others and the pain his actions inflicted on himself, Tom had come to the end of his rope. The hurting had to stop. After unburdening all the terrible memories that his actions had placed in his mind and heart, he understood for the first time that Jesus loved him. Tom responded, and his life was changed. That day he began to turn from pleasing Satan to pleasing God.

Each of us needs to ask ourselves: When will enough be enough? When will we grow tired of hurting ourselves by hurting others, making this world a worse place because of our actions, fear, or lack of character and love? If we follow the crowd like helpless sheep, when will enough be enough?

Sure, you may not be a gang member. But if you're lying to your parents, haven't asked forgiveness from a friend, are taking advantage of someone, are gaining your pleasures at the expense of someone else, or are hurting anyone, it needs to stop. Cry out today, "Enough is enough!"

If you can't say that today, ask yourself: When will it be enough? When will I be able to turn to Jesus? When can the Holy Spirit take over my life? What will make me stop living for myself and begin to stand up for the Creator of the universe?

The time is today. Enough sin has been committed—it's more than enough.

On Christmas day 1978, I knew that enough was enough and asked God to wipe away my sins. The pain was too great to bear anymore. Today, you can say that enough is enough and start on a new path. All it takes is putting your faith in Jesus.

# 24

# Choose Your Last Words Carefully

"Say 'I love you' as your children leave the house for a date, because one time it might be the last time you ever see each other," I counseled parents in one of my seminars.

After the talk, a mother took me off to the side to tell me the importance of those words. Her son had died in a car accident a few years before, and the last thing he did was fight with her over clothes. The argument became loud, and he left the house with anger, pain, and frustration written all over his face. It left the entire family devastated and feeling guilty for letting him leave in such an angry state of emotions.

What words did you say as you last parted from your mom and dad? Would you feel proud to have those burned on their brains as the last words you ever spoke? If you are fortunate enough to have a grandmother and grandfather, what words will they remember that you spoke when you left them?

Someday the words you speak to your loved ones will be your last words. That's why it's important to treat everyone you meet today like the most important person in the world. Leave your friends, family, and even strangers with words of kindness, not bitterness. If you've said the wrong things, get together with that person and apologize. Make it right quickly.

Someday I will give my last speech—I felt the impact of that truth when I thought I'd had a heart attack. So before each talk, I pray that I'd give it as if it might be my last one. That's why I don't talk about fluff; I pull no punches. If I feel my audience needs a strong message about premarital sex because their eyes tell me they started dating too young and they've been used, I challenge each of them to become a secondary virgin—someone who saves himself or herself for a spouse from this moment on.

If my goal, when I speak, is to make Bill Sanders look good, then I don't help teens or their parents. Sure, they may laugh at my jokes or give me a standing ovation, but I haven't influenced their lives.

What were your last words to God? Did you cry out desperately, "Just help me get through this test"? Or did you say, "I love you. I want to spend my time praising you. I'm so blessed to have you as my friend"?

Will people remember you for your loving words or for selfishness? Will you leave a legacy of kindness or disdain?

Never forget the importance of last words.

# 25
# Liar! Murderer!

If you knew that someone was a liar and a murderer, would you want to spend time with him? Would you rearrange your schedule to fit in his favorite activities and ask his advice on the most important matters in your life?

I don't think so! But that's exactly what people do when they follow Satan instead of God. You see, Satan is the Father of Lies, and he's a murderer too. He began by lying to himself and the angels by saying he could be God. As a result, God threw him out of heaven. So Satan brought his cause to earth and lied to Eve, bringing shame to humanity.

Jesus pointed out their true allegiance when some of his own people refused to believe in him:

> You are of your father the devil, and you want to do the desires of your father. He was a murderer from the beginning, and does not stand in the truth, because there is no truth in him. Whenever he speaks a lie, he speaks from his own nature; for he is a liar, and the father of lies.
>
> John 8:44

Like those people in Jesus' day, many today cannot see what the problem is. That's because Satan has made them blind to it: "The god of this world has blinded the minds of the unbelieving, that they might not see the light of the gospel of the glory of Christ, who is the image of God" (2 Cor. 4:4). Paul described Satan as "the spirit that is now working in the sons of disobedience" (Eph. 2:2).

No one is exempt from the wiles of the tempter. He tricked Adam and Eve, and he boldly tempted Jesus: "And the tempter came and said to Him, 'If You are the Son of God, command that these stones become bread'" (Matt. 4:3). He even quoted Scripture in an attempt to sway Jesus.

The apostle Peter, who had firsthand experience in falling under Satan's spell, warned, "Be of sober spirit, be on the alert. Your adversary, the devil, prowls about like a roaring lion, seeking someone to devour" (1 Peter 5:8).

Follow Jesus' example, and know your Scripture well enough to avoid Satan's lies. Let truth and God's Word guard you against the enemy's attack.

# 26
# Lots of Lies but Few Regrets

Teachers I've talked to estimate that 90 percent of their students lie and cheat and show very little regret. One teacher told me, "It's as if teens don't have a conscience anymore."

Hundreds of parents have shared that their young people lie to them while looking them square in the eye. After they lie, these teens will even say, "You can trust me. Don't you believe me?" Or, "What do I have to do to earn your trust?"

Lies will never accomplish anything good in the long run. The worst thing about a lie is that you have to tell more lies to cover it up. Soon you become hardened so that when God calls you to stop telling lies and follow him, you may not even hear him.

Recently we caught my son in a lie. After we punished him, he admitted, "I couldn't concentrate all day at school. It hurt me in my heart. I cried several times, even though no one knew what I was crying about. I'm sorry, Daddy." Brandon had a soft heart toward God. He knew he'd done wrong and felt glad when it was all out in the open.

Everyone makes mistakes—sometimes you can't help doing that. But you get to choose whether or not you will lie. When you decide to lie, you can't blame your choice on a friend. You can say the devil made you do it or blame it on a difficult childhood, but your argument won't be convincing. Instead of lying to cover up a mistake, why not just admit it and get it over with?

Americans have a big lying problem. Athletes who break curfew, drink, smoke, or use drugs know they should be off the team for their actions, but they party anyway. Boys lie to their girlfriends, getting them drunk and telling them they will love them forever, when they are really only seeking to gratify their own pleasures. Girls lie to themselves, doing what they know is wrong because they think a boy can meet their needs.

Write down the names of five people you've lied to in the last three months. Go back to them, look them in the eye, and say, "I'm sorry; I lied." Then tell them the truth. Your actions will make a permanent mark in their minds. They'll know you as a person of integrity and will think more highly of you than ever before. Soon you will also think better of yourself.

When Satan attacked Jesus with lies in the desert, Jesus fought back with Scripture. You can too. When you face trouble, remember that God has said, "Do not lie to one another" (Col. 3:9). It's not a suggestion from God—it's a command. It's just like "Thou shalt not kill."

Lying kills relationships, dreams, and hope. If you lie on the job, you're probably going to be unemployed. If you don't know how to tell the truth about yourself, you'll never be the best you could become.

Once you tell the first lie, it becomes easier to lie the next time. When you watch soap operas and movies that focus on lies, you get the idea that it's really okay to lie. You watch people make millions, and they live a lie. Is it any wonder that it's so hard to find a truthful person in this generation?

If you find that it's easy to lie, pray about this and ask God to put his Spirit in your heart. Ask him to teach you to hate lying, because the one who tempts you to lie is the same devil who causes a father to have sex with his daughter. The Satan who causes you to tell "white lies" also causes doctors to kill unborn babies.

When someone tells you a lie, don't stand for it. Speak out and tell the truth. Refuse to go along with the crowd if they want to do something wrong.

Young men and women of integrity are desperately needed in this world. Be one who can stand up and be counted, who can make a difference in the course of humanity.

Tell the truth. It's a great way to live, and you'll have few regrets on the day you die.

# 27
## Outpoured Love

To help a high-school senior who was dying of cancer, an entire school and community bonded together. They supported the teen, helped his family, and raised money for the escalating medical bills. This outpoured love touched me deeply.

That small town in Ohio lived out the message of Scripture about helping others. The attitude that "we're in this all together" was just what God had in mind.

> For the despairing man there should be kindness from
>   his friend;
> Lest he forsake the fear of the Almighty.
>
> Job 6:14

> Learn to do good;
> Seek justice,
> Reprove the ruthless;
> Defend the orphan,
> Plead for the widow.
> Isaiah 1:17

> You shall not take vengeance, nor bear any grudge against the sons of your people, but you shall love your neighbor as yourself; I am the LORD.
>
> Leviticus 19:18

The classic New Testament story on the subject was told by Jesus when a lawyer asked him, "Who is my neighbor?" Jesus answered with the story of the despised Samaritan who helped the wounded traveler by the side of the road:

Jesus replied and said, "A certain man was going down from Jerusalem to Jericho; and he fell among robbers, and they stripped him and beat him, and went off leaving him half dead. And by chance a certain priest was going down that road, and when he saw him, he passed by on the other side. And likewise a Levite also, when he came to the place and saw him, passed by on the other side. But a certain Samaritan, who was on a journey, came upon him; and when he saw him, he felt compassion, and came to him, and bandaged up his wounds, pouring oil and wine on them; and he put him on his own beast, and brought him to an inn, and took care of him. And on the next day he took out two denarii and gave them to the innkeeper and said, 'Take care of him; and whatever more you spend, when I return, I will repay you.' Which of these three do you think proved to be a neighbor to the man who fell into the robbers' hands?" And he said, "The one who showed mercy toward him." And Jesus said to him, "Go and do the same."

Luke 10:30–37

Jesus didn't say those last words only to the people who listened to him that day. They're meant for you and me.

Let's do it!

# 28

# I'm Not the Man for This

As Christian guitarist Jimmy A. prepared to perform at Wichita Week, the teens in the audience were loud and seemed uninterested in listening to the seven artists and speakers who had come. Jimmy had the tough job of being the opening act.

Before this young artist from Nashville walked onto the stage, he looked back and said to the rest of us who would follow, "I'm not the man for this." Whether or not we admitted it, his words reflected the fear that was crashing in on all of us.

On stage, Jimmy A. did a marvelous job. As a result, his challenging words have stuck with me. When it comes to handling life, saying no to temptations, making the world a better place, being a person of character when life seems valueless, none of us but God is the man for this. We don't have the strength to do anything good by ourselves.

Trying to handle Satan on your own, without God's awesome power, is an overwhelming mistake. Alone, you're not the man for the job. Don't imagine you can single-handedly go through life forgiving people who have harmed you, who have destroyed your hopes and dreams, who have abused you.

You cannot love your enemies on your own. Certain things you cannot do without help. God is the man for it. When troubles come, we need God more than ever. And he is always there, waiting for us to turn to him when we need strength. "O LORD," prayed the prophet Isaiah, "be gracious to us; we long for you. Be our strength every morning, our salvation in time of distress" (Isa. 33:2 NIV).

"I'm not the man for this" should be the lifetime battle cry that we shout when Satan nears us. When temptation stands at our elbow, we need to exclaim, "In the name of Jesus, be gone!"

Don't think that calling for outside reinforcements shows your own weakness. Instead it shows your wisdom and the strength of your relationship with God. Rather than giving Satan an open door, you are slamming it in the destroyer's face. Satan wants to separate us from Jesus any way he can. He tempts us to call God a wimp and think other Christians are nerds. But if you let him walk into your life, he will smash your dreams beyond recognition, lead you down the most negative path life has to offer, and ruin you.

Cling to the cry "I'm not the man for this!" and you can be strong in the power of Jesus. The next time there is good to be done, call on God to help you do it. Ask him to aid you in avoiding the bad. Recognize that you need more love and grace than you could ever come up with alone. Turn to him for the strength and character to overcome.

Just as God was on stage with Jimmy A., he'll go with you today. Alone, you might not be able to say no to cheating on a test, looking at pornography, listening to music that is honoring only to Satan, or continually lying to your parents, but with God you can refuse it.

Never be too ashamed to say, "I'm not the man for this!" You see, it's the truth.

# Only One Life

"What's the matter?" the pastor asked the weeping and shaking seventy-eight-year-old man he was about to baptize. The man had recently accepted Christ and until the last few minutes had seemed overjoyed that he had the Lord in his heart.

Looking at a young boy, the elderly man replied, "This boy has nearly seventy more years than I have to live for the Lord. Oh, how I wish I hadn't wasted my entire life living for myself."

That man had learned the harsh lesson that people's lives are soon gone, turned into vapor. If they've lived for themselves, like this man, they experience regrets.

A business in our town called Chicken Coop not only serves delicious chicken, but on its window and cups it offers a similar message, "Only one life, 'twill soon be past, only what's done for Christ shall last."

"'What will a man be profited, if he gains the whole world, and forfeits his soul? Or what will a man give in exchange for his soul?'" is the way Jesus said it (Matt. 16:26). Every individual has to answer that second question. What will you give in exchange for your soul?

- Pride that will not allow you to overcome the hurt and anger of a bitter childhood?

- Desire to be the coolest guy in school?
- Drive to be the next Michael Jordan?
- Craving for drugs or alcohol?
- Greed to have more money than your parents ever dreamed of?

Some of these may provide temporary satisfaction. But in the end they will all leave you alone and empty. Is that a legacy you'd be proud of?

Only what's done for Christ will last. Don't wake up at seventy-eight and have regrets.

When I play golf, I always think, "No wasted shots!" Losing concentration in the middle of a match makes me swing with only half the effort, and I get only half the shot. So to play well, I must focus on each one.

Your life is much more important than a golf game. Concentrate on having no wasted days or opportunities. Embed in your mind the determination to ask others if they know Christ. When you meet a stranger, ride a bus, or fly, keep a gospel tract on hand and share the Good News.

What will last about your life? Will it be the testimony you gave for Jesus?

# 30

# Do You Pray the Way You Pack?

How do you pack your suitcase? Are you organized or haphazard?

I'm a last-minute packer. It used to drive my wife absolutely crazy. But the other day she said she now knows my style and is even beginning to enjoy it!

When I'm hurrying to catch a plane, my entire family and half the neighbors know it. I keep having this one-sided conversation:

"Honey, where's the strap for my carry-on bag?"
"I'm out of shampoo again."
"Which one of you kids took the batteries for my Walkman?"
"Brandon!" (I heard him lock his door so he won't have to give them up.)
"Get my file, honey, and make sure the tickets are in there."

Halfway out the door, herding the kids toward the van, Holly calls out, "Hurry up or you'll miss this one!"

My mind doesn't even begin to move until I've got barely enough time to catch the plane on a dead run. "Please, oh please, Jesus, don't let me get a flat tire," I'm praying as I drive. At zero hour I have ten minutes left, and it's go, man, go.

I love being on the edge, but sometimes my style affects others. Like the time I walked in minutes before addressing a high school of twenty-four hundred hyper teens, anxiously waiting in the gym. To the nervous principal I quipped, "My accountant would have been here early, but he's boring. So there you go!"

The problem with my packing style isn't my packing style— it's with the way I run my life. I can get away with driving off in the wrong direction and only having a few minutes to spare when I reach my speaking engagement. I can even joke about that when I talk.

But I get in real trouble when I try to pray the way I pack. When I've made the wrong turn and I've only got a few minutes left, it's easy for me to cry out, "Help me just this one time, Lord, and I promise I'll never do anything wrong as long as I or my offspring may live." (Ever notice how easy it is to call God "Lord" when you are scared to death, in trouble, unprepared, or driving seventy-four miles an hour and you realize that through the last three blasting tunes a state cop has been flashing his lights behind you?)

If I continue packing this way, I may miss flights, forget my underwear, or go without shampoo. I can live without the clean clothes and shampoo. But I can't live without God.

Never talk to God except when you're in a jam? Then you probably aren't close to him—and may not even want to be. Don't think you're getting away with something. God knows the difference between those who pray in moments of trouble and those who really want to know him. He warns:

Not everyone who says to Me, "Lord, Lord," will enter the kingdom of heaven; but he who does the will of My Father who is in heaven. Many will say to Me on that day, "Lord, Lord, did we not prophesy in Your name, and in Your name cast out demons, and in Your name perform many miracles?" And then I will declare to them, "I never knew you; depart from Me, you who practice lawlessness."

Matthew 7:21–23

> **God knows the difference between those who pray in moments of trouble and those who really want to know him.**

When you pray, put all your energy and best skills into it. Write down your prayers. Spend a few moments praising God for who he is, admitting your sins and mistakes, requesting that God meet your needs, and thanking him for answers to past prayers and many blessings.

Praise, Admit, Request, and Thank spell out PART. Do your part by talking to God and living for him. He will do his part too.

I'd love to say more about spending time with the Lord in prayer, but I think I just heard my wife yell something about missing a plane!

# 31

## Lost Your Patience? Find It Here!

I read the story of a young father who had no patience with his one-and-a-half-year-old. The crying child confused and angered the dad, and he shook him to stop the crying. He stopped it, all right. The child died in his father's arms.

Something this drastic is unlikely to happen to you, but it could. That dad probably never thought it could happen to him either.

Everyone needs patience, and it seems that when you need it the most, it's hardest to find. You'll never stumble across patience when you're walking aimlessly through the woods. You have to search for it.

The good news is that God has some special hiding places that need not remain secrets to his children. They are the truths hidden in the Scriptures, which tell us:

*When you get patience, you get lots of other goodies too.* "The fruit of the Spirit is love, joy, peace, patience, kindness, goodness, faithfulness, gentleness and self-control" (Gal. 5:22–23). Notice that it's called a fruit. Like any other growing thing, a tree grows fruit only if it's nourished, watered, and well cared for. Are you walking with Jesus today so that you can grow spiritual fruit?

*When you feel God's power close by, you will find it easy to live with patience.* The secret is to stay in the Lord's presence and be "strengthened with all power, according to His glorious might, for the attaining of all steadfastness and patience; joyously" (Col. 1:11).

*As a child of God, you have a special outfit to wear to school today.* It will turn heads like nothing else you've ever worn. People will want to be around you when you're decked out in this. "And so, as those who have been chosen of God, holy and beloved, put on a heart of compassion, kindness, humility, gentleness and patience" (Col. 3:12).

*You have to work at staying patient.* When you are lazy and out of God's Word or desire, you will not please Jesus—and you won't grow in patience. Even though it takes effort, a patient life is definitely worth it. God's Word encourages you "that you may not be sluggish, but imitators of those who through faith and patience inherit the promises" (Heb. 6:12).

*When you come to the end of this rainbow, you will find more than a pot of gold.* The Maker himself will be waiting for you with open arms. Search for patience with all your heart until Jesus comes to take you home. Wait for him: "Be patient, therefore, brethren, until the coming of the Lord. Behold, the farmer waits for the precious produce of the soil, being patient about it, until it gets the early and late rains" (James 5:7). Waiting for Jesus is worth every minute!

Why wait to apply these truths and verses to your life? Patience is so wonderful, and you can have it today.

# 32
## Practice Run

"Why do you spend time challenging students to use seat belts?" I'm often asked. "They already know about that!"

I have a twofold purpose in encouraging teens to buckle up. First, deciding to buckle your seat belt is good decision-making practice. If negative peer pressure has the power to keep you from buckling up, you know that you need to learn to make unpopular choices. If a friend's not using a seat belt sways you so easily, you'll probably have trouble thinking for yourself when it comes to using drugs or alcohol, having premarital sex, cheating, lying, stealing, hurting someone, or gossiping. When someone tells jokes you're not proud of, you will not have the courage to turn away from them, and you may find it easier to use profanity than to clean up your speech.

Seat belts are a perfect practice ground. You use them when you're with your parents and even by yourself, but not when you give your friends a ride. Begin to use your belt when you drive with your friends, and you'll be contagious. When the driver buckles up, so do most of the other people in the car.

My second goal is to help teens start saving lives. Jimmy was a freshman when he suffered brain damage as the result of a car accident. At 3:30 in the afternoon, on the way home from school with his sister, he unbuckled for one minute in order to grab his books from the back of the car. As he went to rebuckle, his sister's car was hit head-on by a car in the hands of a drunk driver. Jimmy's sister had her seat belt on and came through the accident unscathed. Jimmy walks and talks funny and has to wear protective head gear that looks like a football helmet with the back cut out to provide room for his protruding head.

"Wear your seat belts and don't take them off until you are done driving and the car is turned off," advises Jimmy. "Be smart about it. Being too cool for seat belts is like being too stupid to help yourself."

# 33

# Pray Him Out of His Pain

"I'm so frustrated that I can't do anything for him," I shared with some Christian buddies. "He's made choices, and now he's living with the consequences, but I feel as if I were without arms, legs, or voice. I can't seem to help him." The young friend under discussion was behind bars because he had broken the law.

"Pray him out of his pain," one of my friends advised.

"What do you mean?"

"You pray for him hard and often. You pray so much that your friend will feel the effort of your prayers. God will touch his spirit, and somehow he will know someone is praying for him.

"It may change his actions; it may cause him to turn to God; it may cause him to refocus his thoughts and become God-pleasing instead of self-punishing. No matter what, you pray as hard as you can. You will be doing all you can under the circumstances."

When someone is hurting, we need to pray. God does care and will help, if we ask.

Arise, LORD! Lift up your hand, O God.
Do not forget the helpless. . . .
You hear, O LORD, the desire of the afflicted;
you encourage them, and you listen to their cry.
Psalm 10:12, 17 NIV

However, if we pray under these circumstances and never take any action, we are wasting our time. "If anyone has material possessions and sees his brother in need but has no pity on him, how can the love of God be in him? Dear children, let us not love with words or tongue but with actions and in truth" (1 John 3:17–18 NIV). If you can help a person by visiting him in jail, do that. If you know a friend needs clothes, help meet his need.

God doesn't want us to ask him to do anything he has enabled *us* to do. Pray hard, but also look for ways to serve. See how you can make your arms, mouth, or legs work for Jesus.

"For I was hungry and you gave me something to eat, I was thirsty and you gave me something to drink, I was a stranger and you invited me in. . . ." The King will reply, "I tell you the truth, whatever you did for one of the least of these brothers of mine, you did for me."
Matthew 25:35, 40 NIV

When we try to help others, often we want to help them avoid the ultimate pain of hitting rock bottom and having to look up to God. Do this and you may be standing in the way of someone's finding Jesus. Don't help so often and so completely that the hurting person does not feel a need for the ultimate help—the soul's salvation.

Pray hard. Be all you can be. Know that you've done what you could and that there is no more physical action you could take. Then pray the pain out of that person.

Whom can you pray for today? Ease the pain of a lonely classmate by becoming his friend. Erase hurt by showing love and tenderness to a coworker. Pray for your family members, the kid who picks on you every day, or someone you've just met. Whom can you help?

Do this every day to instill in your spirit the knowledge that nothing is impossible with God. Tell yourself, "I don't have to go along with the world's attitudes, be angry because someone else is, or do what everyone else my age does. I can learn to forgive and love, turn the other cheek, and turn frowns into smiles."

Let God live out his desires in your life today. Give him your all. With his strength you can help pray someone, somewhere, out of his pain.

# 34
# Resistance Movement

"It's as if Satan keeps hanging on to me," explained Ed, a young Christian. "It's awful hard to turn away from my past and to the things I know God wants."

I explained to Ed that he was trying to fight Satan in his own power, and if he kept on that way, he would certainly lose. "It's when you turn your face toward God and turn your back on Satan that you are headed in the right direction," I shared.

Like Ed, in God's power you can fight back against Satan. "The Lord is faithful, and He will strengthen and protect you from the evil one" (2 Thess. 3:3). But that doesn't mean you can leave the door wide open, allowing Satan a place in your life. Start your own resistance movement. When Satan tries to take control, fight back.

"Do not give the devil an opportunity" (Eph. 4:27). As much as you can, stay away from the temptations. Don't go to a party where alcohol will be served. Avoid making friends within a crowd that will only get you into trouble.

As you turn from the negative, begin to take positive steps too. "Submit therefore to God. Resist the devil and he will flee from you" (James 4:7).

Be of sober spirit, be on the alert. Your adversary, the devil, prowls about like a roaring lion, seeking someone to devour. But resist him, firm in your faith, knowing that the same experiences of suffering are being accomplished by your brethren who are in the world.

1 Peter 5:8–9

You don't have to take anything Satan wants to dish out. With God as your strength, you can say no to sin. When he knocks on your door, don't open it!

> **With God as your strength,
> you can say no to sin.**

Even when Satan makes you suffer for your faith, know that God has not forgotten your pain. He has prepared a very unpleasant future for that fallen angel:

> Then He will also say to those on His left, "Depart from Me, accursed ones, into the eternal fire which has been prepared for the devil and his angels."
>
> Matthew 25:41

> Now judgment is upon this world; now the ruler of this world [Satan] shall be cast out.
>
> John 12:31

> And He [the Holy Spirit], when He comes, will convict the world . . . concerning judgment, because the ruler of this world has been judged.
>
> John 16:8, 11

> The devil who deceived them was thrown into the lake of fire and brimstone, where the beast and the false prophet are also; and they will be tormented day and night forever and ever.
>
> Revelation 20:10

That's the rest of Satan's story. He and all his followers will spend eternity in the lake of fire. And eternity isn't just a weekend stay—it lasts forever and ever.

So keep up the battle, even when it's not going well. Choose God's side, and take your friends with you. That's the best resistance you can make.

# 35
# Legal Rights and Wrongs

"We know our rights, and we carry our Bibles to class even though it makes our teachers and other students mad at us," announced some students I met recently.

My response probably surprised them. "Do you think what you are doing is leading more people toward Christ?" I asked. "Are you causing more people to thirst and hunger for the Christian lifestyle, or are you using your rights to antagonize and anger others?"

When I said that, I wasn't wimping out. I'm all for Christians knowing their legal rights on a school campus. I hope you know that you can study the Bible with a student-led group or club on school property before or after classes. Christians need to fight for their rights with conviction and backbone.

But in this case, I believed the students were doing more harm than good. So I asked, "Are you carrying these Bibles to school to read? Do you study them? Or do you take them because it brings you more attention and gets you pats on the back by your religious friends?"

These students were bringing attention to God, all right. But they didn't follow Jesus' example or the precept that he gave in Matthew 5:16: "Let your light shine before men in such a way that they may see your good works, and glorify your Father who is in heaven." Jesus wanted to further the work of his Father. When he confronted sinners, he taught them right from wrong and showed them the way they needed to choose—God's way. Getting in their faces wasn't just a way of proving that he had rights. He helped them to know God and live in a way that would please him.

Know your rights, but don't abuse them. Because what you do today could destroy another opportunity. Once I had the doors to a school closed to me because another speaker had been there first and overstepped his boundaries. At the end of the assembly, without permission from the principal, he blurted out the plan of salvation. The principal, teachers, and nonbelievers were all embarrassed. The press had a heyday.

Though that speaker might have been a testimony, I don't believe he was wise. None of the rest of us who would like to challenge those teens to say no to alcohol and other drugs and turn from premarital sex will get the thrill of hearing a student from that school say, "Thank you for coming. Next weekend I was going to give up my virginity, but because of your talk, I am going to hang on to it until my wedding night." The teens there will never have the opportunity to be encouraged by a speaker to make the best choices for their lives.

I'm not saying you shouldn't let people know that you love Jesus. Wear your Christian T-shirt if you want, but be certain you also live out God's message, or your witness will have been useless. Carry a Bible to school, but don't just do it for show. Let people see the point of carrying it when they see you digging into God's Word.

Show your faith for the right reasons, and people will want to be like you. Follow the Lord, and you will glorify him.

# 36

# Rookie!

Michael Jordan had announced that he was trying base-ball! It was the hottest news on the airwaves, and you could pick up many magazines that predicted the gifted athlete would fail in his new venture.

But I loved his attitude. Though he was the hottest thing on the basketball court, he was willing to go back, be a rookie, and try something new. "I'm not afraid to fail, but I refuse not to try!" he exclaimed.

Have you been afraid to learn Scripture, teach Sunday school, become a neurosurgeon, or take up guitar lessons? Then you need to hear Michael's message. What has fear of failure kept you from doing?

A few years ago I went out for the basketball team at our church. During my school years I had feared trying it and only played one year. But I overcame my fear and started play-ing with my church team.

At first I was absolutely the worst player ever. In one game I was guarding my own man after he got a rebound. Every-one else headed to the other end of the floor, and Gary looked at me and said, "Bill, we're going the other way."

For seven or eight years I've been with the church team, and I've improved a lot. I still can't jump, but I have kept doing something I'm not great at. No one will ever applaud me for my talent and court sense, but I work as hard as anyone, and others appreciate my effort.

The other day I met a man in his midthirties who refuses to get into a serious relationship. "I'm not going to take another chance," he insists. "I don't want someone to dump me after I've shared the deepest part of myself. I've been vulnerable, and women have ripped out my heart when they said good-bye.

"I was in love with one woman, and we were going to get married. When it didn't work out, I knew life wasn't fair."

Now this man occupies himself with work. He travels all over the world and has as many hobbies as he can. But he's running away from life and refuses to even try again. Failure licked him, and he has his tail between his legs.

Satan would love to shut you down because of fear. Don't let him do it! When he has you scared, he has you trapped. If you don't want to try that new sport or activity, if you're afraid to share the gospel with someone, you're trapped inside yourself. Perhaps you only stay in one or two areas of life where you know you can excel.

Don't let yourself stop living because you could feel embarrassed at what others think or say. Everyone experiences embarrassment, but no one has to let it take over his life. Even if no one applauds, you will know that you've tried something and grown by doing it.

With the strength God can give you, I challenge you to take on the attitude "I will never again be so afraid to fail that I refuse to try."

Michael Jordan has a winning outlook, and I'd never bet against him. Even though he never made it to the big leagues, he can look himself in the mirror and say, "At least I gave it a try. No matter if the crowds cheered or jeered, I gave it my best. It didn't matter if it was NBA basketball or major league baseball."

Don't let worries about what other people think stop you. The truth is that they will be so busy worrying about themselves they may never notice you. So get on with it—give life a chance.

# 37

# The Final Score

How confident would you be if you already knew the final score of the basketball game you were playing? Remember in one of the *Back to the Future* movies where Biff got hold of a sports trivia book? Because he had gone back in time, he could bet confidently on races and win millions. He knew the final score before the race had been run.

What if you were playing a golf match and knew you'd win by two strokes? Though you might get the lead and lose it a couple of times and even come down to a playoff, you'd know you'd win the game.

I'd like to think that having the idea we'd win would make us play with confidence and kindness. We'd give our all, but if our opponents fell down, we would pick them up. Because nervousness and stress would disappear, we could be kind and gentle.

There's a question that's more important than "Do you know the final score in your upcoming football or basketball game?" It's "Do you know the final score of your life?"

You could ask that question another way: "What is your greatest possession?" Mine is eternal life. If I was crossing the road and a truck hit me, I could die instantly and have confidence that I would be with Christ forever in eternity. For eon upon eon, forever and ever, I would be with God.

Think as far ahead as you can. When that thought is completed, eternity will have just begun. That's lots of time with no pain, tears, meetings, exams, fusses, or fights to interrupt. I'll have no people to console, no letters to answer, no speeches to prepare, no heartaches to mend.

But eternity will also have to do with quality. I can expect a quality of life I only dream of today on earth.

You can have all that too if you turn your life over to Christ.

If you're saying, "I did that, but I don't have your peace and confidence, Bill," you've lost sight of the final score. You are acting as if you can only lose in the end, when God has said you will win. You are saying the temptations are too strong, when Christ has already empowered you to say no.

Even if you haven't read it, the final page is already written. Since God knows the future and has told you what to expect, count on him. Today make the right choices, knowing that if you've trusted in Christ, you can live with confidence and kindness.

**Today make the right choices, knowing that if you've trusted in Christ, you can live with confidence and kindness.**

Enjoy life, knowing that you've seen the ending. Don't take people for granted or play games to get in with the wrong crowd so you can feel special. If you are born again, you have something better than that. God has already taken care of the final score. Someday Satan and his demons will be thrown into the lake of fire. Trust in that and live as if you really believe it.

Don't settle for second best. God's already given you first place!

# 38

# Everyone Sees Your Sermon

If you are a Christian, every day you live is a sermon to someone. It may be a bad sermon or a good one, but those who know of your faith will read it in the things you do.

The Bible describes the same thing when it calls Christians a city on a hill. Our light shines into the surrounding countryside, whether or not the neighbors like it.

I experienced this truth a while ago, when some friends and I had a week-long speaking engagement. As we prayed one day, we realized that our audience wasn't just the assembly of teens or the parents we spoke to each evening. Every day we came in contact with people. The same driver took us to and from each engagement. People set up our sound equipment and helped us carry in our books and cassettes. At the hotel we met the staff members: secretaries, people at the desk, and the restaurant crew. Guests also saw us around the hotel.

Our attitude toward all those people was more important than the words we spoke. After all, it's easy to get on stage and say one thing and walk off and do another. If we didn't live out what we said, people would ignore our words.

It's the same with you at school and elsewhere in your life. You contact people who watch your life. What they see can

106

eliminate you from the ranks of the hypocrites or place you firmly in their numbers.

As you go to your youth group meeting, don't ignore the elderly person in the parking lot who needs a kind word or the new kid in town who would love to have you invite him. When you walk down the hall in your Christian T-shirt, don't forget to ask a lonely person to have lunch with you.

Once I heard a special message from a Christian who had a reputation as a great prayer warrior. He had written books on prayer. But before the meeting, I noticed he got needlessly upset over the placement of the podium. It wasn't a very good witness to me, and I had to doubt anything he might say about prayer's ability to ease one's stress level.

Every day, even though you might not step to the microphone, you present a sermon, challenging people to give their lives over to God. Make certain you help them hear that message loud and clear.

# 39
# Run from Sex Sin

"The Bible doesn't have anything to say to us today." You may hear that, but don't you believe it. Maybe the people who say that just don't like what they're hearing.

Talk about sex—the Bible has a lot to say:

Flee immorality. Every other sin that a man commits is outside the body, but the immoral man sins against his own body.

1 Corinthians 6:18

But because of immoralities, let each man have his own wife, and let each woman have her own husband.

1 Corinthians 7:2

Therefore consider the members of your earthly body as dead to immorality, impurity, passion, evil desire, and greed, which amounts to idolatry.

Colossians 3:5

For this is the will of God, your sanctification; that is, that you abstain from sexual immorality.

1 Thessalonians 4:3

God says to run from sexual sin—take off, make tracks, split, scram, escape, make a getaway, skip town, skedaddle, vamoose, retreat, withdraw, run for it, turn tail, show a clean pair of heels, depart, or as Snagglepuss, a cartoon character I used to watch, would say, "Exit, stage left, even."

When it comes to avoiding sex sin, God doesn't say walk away, he says, "Get out of town! Flee, brother, flee." But why? Is God in an eternal bad mood? Is he trying to keep teens from having fun? Or does he (oh, I know this sounds like an adult!) know something we don't know?

Look at the last part of 1 Corinthians 6:18 in the Living Bible version: "No other sin affects the body as this one does. When you sin this sin it is against your own body."

All sin affects our walk with God, and many sins hurt our relationships with others, but sexual sin is an act against our own bodies. Though I don't fully comprehend all this verse implies, I know firsthand that God is right. Sexual sin affects you in a way lying, stealing, cheating, doing drugs, showing disrespect, disobeying, and cursing will not. God has said, "Therefore what God has joined together, let man not separate" (Matt. 19:6 NIV). Every time you have sex outside marriage, you destroy part of yourself by making that separation.

Let me illustrate: Sex is a bonding agent—the glue that holds the intimacies of marriage together. If you don't take care of a bottle of glue and leave off the top, it hardens and is ruined. You can't stick anything with it. It's the same with your sex life.

> **Sex outside God's plan is not called *safe*—it's called *sin*. It is a rip-off.**

Or stick a piece of duct tape on your arm. Pull it off. It takes your hair with it. Stick it back on and do it again. It hurts even less this time. By the third or fourth time, it doesn't hurt at all. That's because the adhesive is depleted.

Sex outside God's plan is not called *safe*—it's called *sin*. It is a rip-off. If you stuck your tongue to a frozen ice-cube tray, then pulled it away, it would rip off part of your tongue with it. That's what having sex outside of marriage will do to you.

Sex is more than holding hands—it's the joining of two souls. Jesus described it: "But at the beginning of creation God made them male and female. For this reason a man will leave his father and mother and be united to his wife, and the two will become one flesh. So they are no longer two, but one" (Mark 10:6–8 NIV).

You see, when sex occurs, you become one with that person. That's why rape is so damaging to a woman. The violator didn't just steal a kiss; he stole some of her. He ripped her apart. But you don't have to be raped to suffer. Teens who agree to have sex and later break up feel awful about themselves and the way they have allowed others to treat them.

God says to run from sex outside of marriage, and he calls it a sin. A person who disobeys calls God a liar, betrays his body (which, for a Christian, is the temple of the Holy Spirit), and destroys part of another person.

Outside of marriage, sex is selfish. People who sell sex, such as advertisers, pimps, prostitutes, and abusers, are very sick and selfish.

Don't be foolish in God's eyes. Wise up. Speaking in Proverbs 1:22, Wisdom says, "You simpletons! . . . How long will you go on being fools? How long will you scoff at wisdom and fight the facts?" (TLB).

Even if you don't like what the Bible says, listen and learn from it. That's how you can avoid the most destructive sin of our day.

# 40
# Sodom, California

"Sodom, California? I've never heard of a town called Sodom except in the Bible," you may be thinking. "And it wasn't in California!"

The Sodom of the Bible was a bad place, filled with sin, homosexuality, and wickedness. In fact, it became so bad that God destroyed the city with fire and brimstone. (No, I don't know what brimstone is, but I'm pretty sure I wouldn't want any hitting me on the head, especially if God threw it all the way from heaven.)

"And the Lord said, 'The outcry of Sodom and Gomorrah is indeed great, and their sin is exceedingly grave,'" reports Genesis 18:20. The people were so bad that Abraham pleaded with God to save the city if he could find fifty good and righteous ones. Unsure that there were so many, Abraham kept whittling down the number—forty-five, forty, thirty, twenty, down to ten. If ten people in the city had loved good more than evil, God would have saved it.

But God could not find ten good people there. So he sent angels to warn Lot, Abraham's nephew, and his family. The angels prepared to spend the night in the city square, but Lot invited them to stay in his home.

But he [Lot] was very urgent, until at last they [the angels] went home with him, and he set a great feast before them, complete with freshly baked unleavened bread. After the meal, as they were preparing to retire for the night, the men of the city . . . surrounded the house and shouted to Lot, "Bring out those men to us so we can rape them."

Genesis 19:3–5 TLB

Pretty sick stuff, huh?

The truth is that today is just as sick as the age of Sodom. Focus on the Family sent me a news release from Hamilton Square Baptist Church in San Francisco. During the September 19, 1993, Sunday evening service, one hundred rioters of the gay activist groups Act-Up and Queer Nation surrounded the church, screamed obscenities, and roughed up parishioners who were trying to attend the service. When protesters saw boys and girls inside the church, they shouted, "We want your children. Give us your children."

"They are after me. It's me they want," cried a nine-year-old boy hysterically.

The pastor, Dr. David Innes, begged for additional police support, but the request was denied. He was told, "You must understand. This is San Francisco." No arrests were made.

They call it San Francisco, but it sounds a lot like another city I've heard about.

# 41
## Taking a Stand

On numerous talk shows, A. C. Green of the Phoenix Suns has spoken out for abstinence, saying things like, "I am saving myself for marriage," "True love really does wait," and, "Respect for your future bride is worth it!" Like me, he believes your future wife is worth waiting for.

Though his program Athletes for Abstinence doesn't get a lot of press, isn't on television, and won't be applauded by many groups or organizations, A. C. Green is a man with a cause. Organizations like Planned Parenthood might label his outlook old-fashioned, archaic, or ostrichlike thinking. But his stand will also help you avoid AIDS, keep your girlfriend from becoming pregnant, and leave you both with your self-respect.

When A. C. stands for morality, he doesn't stand alone. Reggie White, an All-Pro lineman for the Green Bay Packers, stood up to be counted. "A lot of people say I was crazy for withdrawing my name from the list for the award for lineman of the year. But I did it. And I would gladly withdraw it again as long as the event is sponsored by an alcoholic beverage company. What they stand for and what I stand for don't even come close to mixing."

You might be saying, "If I were a huge, muscular football player, making millions, I'd take that kind of stand too."

113

I don't believe so. As my friend Pastor Perry Sanders from Lafayette, Indiana, says, "If you can't make the stand now, you won't make it then. If you are not big enough to do little things, you're probably already too little to do big things."

God never allows you to face a temptation you cannot say no to. He'll never let you be put in a position you can't get out of. You may push yourself beyond your level of endurance, but if you do, don't blame anyone else.

Avoiding temptation starts with a conviction. It's knowing that we are special and made in God's image that helps you avoid sex with all the other girls and save yourself for your lifelong partner. It's a conviction that alcohol is the number-one killer of teens and that you will not support it that keeps you away from the booze party.

Don't believe the lies. Refuse to be taken in by the advertising. Don't wear a T-shirt that glamorizes alcohol.

You may not receive applause for your stand. A. C. Green and Reggie White don't get their fair share either. But those men sleep at night, and I'll bet each likes the person he sees in the mirror.

How have you been sleeping lately?

# 42

# It's "Normal" for Teenage Boys

I couldn't believe my ears! A so-called youth expert was telling a mother that it is normal for teenage boys to act on their lust for girls. Let's pick up on their conversation and eavesdrop a little.

The mother said, "My daughter has been wounded and scarred by her boyfriend. He makes her look at pornography with him while he masturbates. She is so confused. She thinks she is in love with him, and he is definitely in control of her. He says he is a Christian and that since he isn't having sex, it's all right. I only found out about this because she got so depressed over it that she went for counseling and finally confided in me."

The youth expert replied, "It's normal for boys to act out their frustrations. After all, they are full of hormones and God says they can't have sex. It is unfortunate that your daughter was hurt by this, but it would have been worse if he had gone all the way with her."

The only thing this man was an expert in was distorting the truth! Let's take a look at some of God's thoughts on lust, and you decide who is wiser, God or today's society.

"But I tell you that anyone who looks at a woman lustfully has already committed adultery with her in his heart" (Matt. 5:28 NIV). Did you hear that? The word is *look*. If you undress a girl with your eyes, you are doing the same thing as sleeping with her. The sin of lust is equal to adultery! Whatever you let your heart and mind dwell on takes control of you. If you are a Christian, please live out your beliefs and act different than this world that makes billions off of lust.

Learn to look at people's faces, not at the rest of their bodies. If a girl dresses provocatively, attracting every passing guy's stare, she is probably in desperate need for attention. Inward pain almost always causes an obsession for outward attention. Don't add to it. Show respect.

Here's another verse: "It is God's will that you should be sanctified: [*Sanctified* means set apart as special for God, to act different from a sin-filled world.] that you should avoid sexual immorality; [Here is proof that your hormones don't have to control you.] that each of you should learn to control his own body in a way that is holy and honorable, not in passionate lust like the heathen, who do not know God" (1 Thess. 4:3–5 NIV). You are commanded to control *your* body, not *hers!* People who are headed toward an eternity without God are called heathen. They act on their lusts. If you are God's child, you know better and you have the power to live a holy life pleasing to him.

God tells you what to do with lust: "Put to death, therefore, whatever belongs to your earthly nature: sexual immorality, impurity, lust, evil desires and greed, which is idolatry" (Col. 3:5 NIV). God commands us to kill our lusts, to get rid of them. Don't read pornography! Don't put in front of your eyes anything you would be ashamed to show your parents, read in front of your church, or have printed on the front page of the newspaper. Be a man of integrity. Treat your girlfriend with respect.

Lust comes from the father of lies, Satan:

For everything in the world—the cravings of sinful man, the lust of his eyes and the boasting of what he has and does—comes not from the Father but from the world. The world and its desires pass away, but the man who does the will of God lives forever.

1 John 2:16–17 NIV

Notice some key words in this verse and ask yourself some questions. "Cravings." Do you crave girls, sex, pornography, or dirty stories? "Lust of the eyes." How many girls do you make feel dirty by staring at their bodies? Instead, do you ever look at them and wonder if they have Jesus in their hearts? You could be the one to tell them about God and his pure love and forgiveness for them.

Do you know a girl who is so in need of love that she will let most any boy take advantage of her? Would you take advantage of her? I hope not. I hope you are taking my challenge of being a man of integrity and honor to heart.

How to treat girls with respect:

*Never turn the lights out!* "Let us behave decently, as in the daytime, not in orgies and drunkenness, not in sexual immorality" (Rom. 13:13 NIV). Have you ever noticed how many sins are committed in the dark? Think about it. When do most robberies, rapes, and murders take place? After dark. Thousands of teens have told me of the sexual scars they carry, and almost all of them took place alone with someone in the dark and in a place they shouldn't have been. It's pretty simple, isn't it? Keep the lights on.

*Don't hang around with Fast Freddie.* "But now I am writing you that you must not associate with anyone who calls himself a brother but is sexually immoral. . . . With such a man do not even eat" (1 Cor. 5:11 NIV). Friends influence friends. If your best friend is Fast Freddie, who only goes to youth group to pick up girls and is so backslidden that the heels of his shoes are worn off, you are disobeying God by hanging around with him, and you're probably taking on the same reputation. Jesus hung around with sinners so he could give salvation to them, not to enjoy their lusts.

A real friend confronts his brother in love and challenges him to confess his sin and get right with God. Be that friend to someone deep in the grip of lust. And beware: Satan will go after you. You are throwing a life raft of truth to someone who is drowning in his lustful desires. Satan doesn't give up that easily.

*Stay away from booze.* "Do not get drunk on wine, which leads to debauchery. Instead, be filled with the Spirit" (Eph. 5:18 NIV). To *debauch* is to corrupt someone, to lead someone off the right track. It starts with alcohol. Think of the stories of some of the booze parties some of your friends, or maybe even you, have thrown. In the midst of all the fun someone is almost always taken advantage of. Some girl gets drunk and someone sleeps with her. She doesn't even remember it until she gets pregnant. The scenarios are endless. Someone almost always leaves with scars. Don't be a part of hurting someone for your own pleasure.

*Develop self-control and self-discipline.* I've found a verse that ties together our need to keep the lights on and our need to stay away from booze. It tells us that if we walk in the light of God's presence we will be exercising self-control:

> You are all sons of the light and sons of the day. We do not belong to the night or to the darkness. So then, let us not be like others, who are asleep, but let us be alert and self-controlled. For those who sleep, sleep at night, and those who get drunk, get drunk at night. But since we belong to the day, let us be self-controlled, putting on faith and love as a breastplate, and the hope of salvation as a helmet.

> 1 Thessalonians 5:5–8 NIV

You do not belong to Satan and the night! Don't accept anything less than God's best for you. God's way is a narrow road and only the strong will travel it. Be strong! Dedicate your life, expecially your sex life, to God. Develop self-control starting today.

You can do it. And if anyone ever says that it's normal for boys to act on their lust and hurt themselves and others, show them what God has to say about it.

# 43

# Superstars

"Do you think God made you this talented just so you could throw a football better than anyone else and have people notice you in the hallways?" I asked my friend Ryan. Mimicking the kid on *Home Alone*, I answered my own question, "I don't think so!"

Ryan is talented and popular. People look up to him. But popularity isn't anything unless you use it the right way. That's why that night after I spoke with his youth group, I challenged Ryan to make bold statements with his life.

"Without giving one speech, you could do a lot because of your popularity. You see, even your softest words and slightest actions stand out to people because they look up to you.

"That's why you don't need to tell your friends to help the school be a kinder place. You just have to find a kid who isn't too popular and sit next to him. Show him a little kindness, and you can pass on that attitude to others.

"If you see someone looking for a seat before the assembly starts, call out, 'Bob, come up here with us,' and you will be imitating Jesus. Your little acts of compassion could save the lives of some lonely teens," I reminded him.

I spoke to Ryan out of personal experience. You see, when I was in high school, I dreamed of being with the "in" crowd. I would have given almost anything to be one of the jocks, but I didn't have Ryan's talent. Instead I tried to act funny in order to be accepted. Sometimes I acted pretty stupid. After making a fool of myself many times, I felt rejected and walked away.

Based on my experience, today I tell teens to look for other kids who share their interests and who also need friends. I'd never encourage teens to choose the "in" crowd if it wasn't for them.

As I looked into Ryan's eyes and gave him that challenge, I realized why it was so important to me. My mind floated back to my freshman year, the day a senior tripped me when I was headed for lunch. As I lay there on the floor, he led ten other upperclassmen into the cafeteria, laughing as they ran over me. Though that experience only lasted a few seconds, twenty-five years later I can still vividly remember it.

I realized that Ryan could have saved me from such humiliation had he been in my school back then. With his courage, he could have pointed out that these guys really weren't so big and mighty if they had to laugh at a skinny kid lying in the dust on the school floor. Perhaps he would have asked me—someone who had nothing to offer but sincere friendship—to sit with him during the big game.

On my way home I thought, "Ryan could turn his school upside down for goodness, gentleness, and kindness. He might notice a depressed teen and stop a suicide before it happens. Ryan could challenge his best friend to stop drinking—and go to his parents if he doesn't. He could turn himself in if he drinks at a party, even though he might get cut from the team."

I have a lot of hopes for Ryan. I hope he will save himself for his future wife and say no to every opportunity for premarital sex. I also hope he'll treat his family with respect, even if he is an upperclassman who hears a lot about his own greatness.

"Why did you put so much pressure on him?" I asked myself as I pulled into my driveway. Had I held up an impossible goal?

"He is hero material," my mind answered. Then it hit me: You are all hero material. Everything I said to Ryan, I want to say to you. You have the ability to be a superstar in God's eyes. Ryan's source of strength can be yours.

As you make bold statements to your world, in your own special way, you can follow the perfect example:

> Your attitude should be the kind that was shown us by Jesus Christ, who, though he was God, did not demand and cling to his rights as God, but laid aside his mighty power and glory, taking the disguise of a slave and becoming like men. And he humbled himself even further, going so far as actually to die a criminal's death on a cross.
>
> Philippians 2:5–8 TLB

You see, superstars aren't just the people with the physical or mental talents. In God's eyes, they are the ones who are willing to become his servants, humbling themselves so that others can become strong in him.

So go out and be a superstar today!

# Teaching the Rules

A gang called the Spur Posse, from Lakeland, California, made national news in 1993 when they were accused of raping and taking advantage of hundreds of girls—some as young as ten years old. Eric Richardson, one of the gang members, told *The New York Times*, "They pass out condoms, teach sex education, and pregnancy-this and pregnancy-that. But they don't teach us any rules."

Hundreds of teens tell me the same thing every year.

Because we all feel more secure when we have guidelines, people need rules. Studies have shown that when fences protect them, kindergartners play better, roaming all over the area. When there are no fences, the children cluster close together in the middle of the playground. They feel frightened.

The Spur Posse gang members did as they pleased, not caring if they ruined lives by leaving girls with nightmares that would not go away. No one had adequately given these boys the message that there is a rule and a Ruler. It had to become a media event before anyone expressed outrage at their actions.

These characterless bullies need to know about the Ruler of the universe and his wisdom-filled guidelines that would have kept them from evil. Had they known these, each might have avoided becoming part of a gang that led him into such sin.

Do not be misled: "Bad company corrupts good character."

1 Corinthians 15:33 NIV

He who walks with the wise grows wise,
    but a companion of fools suffers harm.
Proverbs 13:20 NIV

You adulterous people, don't you know that friendship with the world is hatred toward God? Anyone who chooses to be a friend of the world becomes an enemy of God.

James 4:4 NIV

How I wish these teens had fathers and mothers who lived in a way that stirred their sons to please God rather than themselves. These youths desperately needed to learn right from wrong and understand that they would have to pay a price for breaking the rules.

If you love me, you will obey what I command.
John 14:15 NIV

He who scorns instruction will pay for it,
    but he who respects a command is rewarded.
Proverbs 13:13 NIV

Not everyone who says to me, "Lord, Lord," will enter the kingdom of heaven, but only he who does the will of my Father who is in heaven.

Matthew 7:21 NIV

As they spend many years in prison, these fellows will probably wish they'd been given God's set of rules on sexual morality. How much pain could have been avoided had they known these rules:

Do you not know that the wicked will not inherit the kingdom of God? Do not be deceived: Neither the sexually immoral nor idolaters nor adulterers nor male prostitutes nor homosexual offenders nor thieves nor the greedy nor drunkards nor slanderers nor swindlers will inherit the kingdom of God.

1 Corinthians 6:9–10 NIV

You have heard that it was said, "Do not commit adultery." But I tell you that anyone who looks at a woman lustfully has already committed adultery with her in his heart.

Matthew 5:27–28 NIV

For out of the heart come evil thoughts, murder, adultery, sexual immorality. . . . These are what make a man "unclean."

Matthew 15:19–20 NIV

These teens were in deep need of rules. Where were all the rule givers in their lives? Why did no one spur them on to good deeds instead of evil ones?

# 45
## Just Tell It

Though Dave claims he's a Christian, you'll never see a smile on his face. He doesn't seem to have a purpose, and his light never shines. Not many people would guess that he has any faith in God, since he doesn't tell anyone about it.

You've probably met teens like Dave, and maybe you've wondered what their problem was. I believe they feel so glum because they're not doing what God wants them to do. Because they aren't in God's will, Christians like this don't feel at all fulfilled.

Don't be that way! God meant believers to be full of life, not misery. The secret to an upbeat lifestyle was outlined by Jesus in Acts 1:8 when he told his disciples: "You shall be My witnesses." With those words, he commanded his believers to tell, through word and deed, what it meant to know God. Their lives would give a testimony to the things God can do.

Whether or not we realize it, everyone witnesses to the things that are most important in life. For some people it's a girlfriend or a new car. How do you know what's most important in someone's life? He talks about it, lives it, and breathes it.

It's the same with God. Do you realize that if we talked about the Lord in our everyday conversation, it would show he was on our hearts and minds and that we spent time with him? He would be foremost in our lives, and everyone would know it. When you're excited about something, you can't help talking about it. You share it with other people.

**When you're excited about something, you can't help talking about it.**

At various times about a dozen people have come up to me and said, "I heard about you from your friend Kevin." Because he was excited about our friendship and the things I was doing, Kevin always shared with others about his good friend Bill Sanders, who writes books and speaks to teenagers.

Kevin was proud of me, so he shared the news of our friendship with others—and he shared it positively. Being as close as we are, he knows plenty of bad stuff he could have mentioned. Instead, he built me up in others' eyes, so when they met me they smiled and said, "Oh, yeah, I know you. Kevin's talked about you." Boy, did that make me feel good!

Don't you think it would make God feel good if he heard you talking positively about him to other people?

Now, I don't mean you need to slap people in the face with your Bible or wear a Christian T-shirt everywhere you go. Nor do you have to become so religious that you stop being human. God doesn't want that.

Jesus went where the sinners lived so he could tell them about a new way of life. He talked about God and lived out an exemplary life. When these down-and-out folks believed in him, they found the peace and fullness few had even dreamed of.

Being just like Jesus is our goal. That means we live with excitement, love, joy, and peace. Our eyes sparkle, and we treat people with care and speak of them with love. We live out our love every day—just the way he did. We go to people where they are and show them the new life offered by God.

Being a witness for Christ means our lives speak even louder than our words. But if we have no words, we lack excitement. Get a new pair of jeans or new tennies, and you'll talk about it! If your parents get a new boat or buy a new house, they announce it to all their friends and invite them over. They're not afraid to tell everyone what they've done.

Maybe we don't get that excited about God's great gift to us because it is free. But a very high price was paid, even though we didn't have to come up with any cash. Jesus paid for our souls with his life.

Would you risk some embarrassment to go out on a limb for him? If you have doubts, think of what you should do in a new light. Suppose you were in a crowd of starving people and you knew where to get an endless supply of free bread. You would tell others about that source. Today many people are starving spiritually—though they never tell you about their need. God has shown you the answer. Be a witness today to that starving world.

Not every Christian is too cowardly to stand up for God. One girl in Ohio invited over eighty kids to her church and led several to salvation in Jesus in her senior year of high school. She was putting her faith into action.

In another school, a boy carried a New Testament in his pocket. One day three bullies cornered him and threatened, "You sissy, religion is for sissies. Don't ever bring that Bible back to this school."

The small boy handed the Bible to the biggest bully and spoke lovingly: "Here, see if you have enough courage to carry this around school for one day."

Standing up for Jesus by telling others of him or doing right takes plenty of courage. You have to be strong to say:

"I choose not to drink."
"I decided to save myself for my marriage partner."
"I don't cheat on tests."
"I will obey my parents."

In our world, it isn't cool to do right. A cool person usually talks about his wheels or brags about getting his name in the paper. Rarely will you hear someone publicly standing up for God.

But God is looking for people who will go out on a limb for him. The Bible says God is a jealous God; he doesn't want to share us with other gods: girlfriends, popularity, the need to be noticed, or pride and ego.

You won't gain long-term happiness from the girl you date, the attention you receive on the football field, or being voted most likely to succeed. Jesus recognized how quickly those things fade when he said, "And how does a man benefit if he gains [the popularity of] the whole world and loses his soul in the process?" (Mark 8:36 TLB).

Having Christ in your life and never sharing him is sad. That's why Christians who hide their faith have little to be happy about. But you can be happy by sharing what God's already done for you. As a bonus, when your friends accept Jesus, you'll also know you can be with them for eternity.

# 46
## Total Control?

I don't pick up hitchhikers. Why not? Because my wife asked me not to.

When I tell people that, some say Holly is controlling me. They object even more when I tell them I won't go into bars because of my commitment to her and that I call her once or twice a day when I'm traveling.

Why do I keep on doing all these things? Because I love her and don't want her to lose sleep worrying because she doesn't know what I'm doing.

Even though a lot of people think I'm wrong, I know God doesn't. He tells me that it's natural to please Holly and that I'm supposed to love and enjoy her:

> But one who is married is concerned about the things of the world, how he may please his wife.
>
> 1 Corinthians 7:33

> Husbands, love your wives, just as Christ also loved the church and gave Himself up for her.
>
> Ephesians 5:25

> Enjoy life with the woman whom you love all the days of your fleeting life which He has given to you under the

sun; for this is your reward in life, and in your toil in which you have labored under the sun.

Ecclesiastes 9:9

All these decisions about what I will not do were made to please my wife and help her not to worry about me. Holly isn't being unreasonable when she asks me not to enter a bar; you see, drinking nearly ruined our marriage years ago. Because I also was unfaithful to her, she has reason not to want me to pick up hitchhikers.

If I want to please God, I must remain faithful to Holly. "And the man said, 'This is now bone of my bones, and flesh of my flesh; she shall be called Woman, because she was taken out of Man'" (Gen. 2:23). "You shall not commit adultery" (Exod. 20:14).

I know what happens when I'm in the wrong place doing the wrong thing for the wrong reason. I know my weak areas. So I don't give my wife cause for concern or myself an opportunity to fall. If I follow God's exact commands, I can avoid lots of pain for myself and my wife.

Do you know what your weak points are? Have you made commitments to keep on the path that pleases God? You see, that way God can have total control of your life. It's the most freeing thing in the world.

# 47
## A Trained Eye

When time allows, I love to hunt arrowheads. A couple of years ago in Mississippi, I went out with my cousin Johnny Carson (not the famous TV star). Because he had been to the same spot many times, he knew right where to go. He knew the perfect fields to check after the farmers had just plowed or after a rain, when the arrowheads protruded from the earth.

Each of us had a stick in hand so we could push a stone aside or roll over some dirt to see if an arrowhead lay beneath. The first few times we went out, I noticed that Johnny found more than I did. He'd put his stick to the ground and say, "Look to the left of the stick, two inches." There was a little, red piece of clay. I'd reach down and turn over a two-inch-long spear tip. The last person to touch it was probably a Native American, possibly over a thousand years ago. What excitement to find one of those!

As Johnny taught me, I realized that I needed a trained eye to spot arrowheads.

In life you need a trained eye—someone who is wiser than you, a person with a heart for God, a sensitive eye and ear, and wisdom, who can point you in the right direction. If you want to climb a mountain, you don't hang around people who are afraid of heights. If you want to know how to study, you don't ask a drop-out. If you want to be wise, you have to walk with people who are wiser than you. Place yourself near the people whose training will help you grow.

Today, start finding people with a trained eye—people who know where they are going and whose God is Jesus Christ. Meet people who have a destiny and purpose to make this world a better place. Find those who are willing to stand for integrity.

People around you can be that trained eye, but until you find a human guide, look to God, the ultimate source of wisdom, leadership, and direction. By following the ultimate leader, Jesus Christ, you can become a leader worth following. So listen for his voice before you make your choice: "When he has brought out all his own, he goes on ahead of them, and his sheep follow him because they know his voice. . . . My sheep listen to my voice; I know them, and they follow me" (John 10:4, 27 NIV).

When God provides you with a trained eye, look in the same direction. Listen to the way your guide speaks, and talk in the same way. Follow your guide, who has trained himself to look at Jesus. Then, instead of kicking around in the dirt on your own and missing all the arrowheads, you'll find what you're looking for.

# 48
# End the Violence!

"Violence is killing thousands of children every year in our spiritually sick nation." You'd expect a statement like that from a devotional book, but I read it on the front page of *USA Today*.

Even the liberal press has a clue about the spiritual shape of our nation. The headline read, "Gunshot Kills One U.S. Child Every Two Hours," and the statistics that followed were grim:

- Murder is now the third leading cause of death among children five to fourteen.
- A U.S. child is fifteen times more likely to be killed by a gun than a child in war-torn Northern Ireland.
- From 1979–1991 nearly 50,000 children were killed by guns—almost the number of deaths that occurred in Vietnam.

Then the paper called for parents and other adults to speak out on "the breakdown of spiritual values" and accept responsibility to morally guide, parent, and protect the young.

I believe the paper is right—we are a spiritually sick nation. But I also know that God is the great healer. We need him today more than at any time in history.

To be a great nation, we need these keys set out by Moses in Deuteronomy 4 (NIV). Decide for yourself if America has held on to them.

*Wisdom.* "I have taught you decrees and laws . . . that you may follow them. . . . Observe them carefully, for this will show your wisdom and understanding to the nations, who will hear about all these decrees and say, 'Surely this great nation is a wise and understanding people'" (vv. 5–6). We obtain wisdom by obeying God's laws, and when we do that, people notice.

*Nearness to God.* Moses asked the Israelites, "What other nation is so great as to have their gods near them the way the LORD our God is near us whenever we pray to him?" (v. 7). As we pray and obey God, we draw very close to him.

*Possession of God's laws.* "And what other nation is so great as to have such righteous decrees and laws as this body of laws I am setting before you today?" (v. 8). God's laws are not to be ignored or mocked, for they are good, righteous rules for living.

*Acceptance of a final authority.* "Do not add to what I command you and do not subtract from it, but keep the commands of the LORD your God that I give you" (v. 2). God's Word is the final authority. A wise nation will not try to get around it but will obey every part of it.

**God's Word is the final authority.**

*Obedience to the law.* "He declared to you this covenant, the Ten Commandments, which he commanded you to follow" (v. 13). Without obedience, the law is useless.

*Turning from idols.* "Therefore watch yourselves very carefully, so that you do not become corrupt and make for yourselves an idol" (vv. 15–16). A wise nation fixes its eyes on God and will not be distracted by worldly pleasures or temptations.

*Godly education.* "Assemble the people before me to hear my words so that they may learn to revere me as long as they live in the land and may teach them to their children" (v. 10). People who know God can pass faith on. A nation devoted to God learns all it can of him.

*Trusting God's protection.* "Keep his decrees and commands, which I am giving you today, so that it may go well with you and your children after you and that you may live long in the land the LORD your God gives you for all time" (v. 40). Obedience to God and trust in him ensures a nation's well-being.

*Recognizing God as God.* "Acknowledge and take to heart this day that the LORD is God in heaven above and on the earth below. There is no other" (v. 39). Giving God his place in this world will make a nation prosper.

Even if the world and our country don't follow God's rules, you can do it in your own life. The choices you make as a result of your faith will strengthen your family and community—and eventually it may even reach the nation.

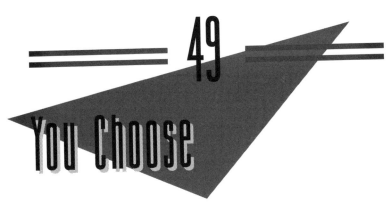

## You Choose

Dear Bill,

I've been told "Like father, like son," so many times that I believe it. Is it true?

My dad was abused as a child. My grandpa is a mean man, and we never go near him. From ages three to six I was abused. Now I'm seventeen, and through counseling, all the memories of the abuse have come back to me.

I don't want to follow in my father's steps, but people tell me that children of abusers grow up to be abusers when they have kids.

Is it true? How can I make sure I don't do to others what he did to me?

Discouraged but Hopeful

An alcoholic father had identical twin sons who were taken from him at age two and put in a foster home because he was an unfit and dangerous parent. When they were twenty-five, the two children were interviewed. One had become a troubled alcoholic just like his father. The other had a happy, successful family life and never touched a drop of alcohol.

"How did you become like this?" the interviewer asked both.

From both he got the same reply, "What would you expect, with a father like mine?"

The answer is simple, Discouraged but Hopeful—the choice is yours. You are not tied into the cycle your family has fallen into. By making your own decisions, you can change the pattern in your family and in your own life.

Follow this three-step formula for family change, based on Ezekiel 18:14, 17 (TLB): "But if this sinful man has, in turn, a son who sees all his father's wickedness, so that he fears God and decides against that kind of life, . . . he [the son] shall surely live."

Step 1: *Clearly see your father's sins.* Realize the pain he is in. Understand—as I'm sure you do all too well—the agony caused by his abuse or wickedness. See the tormenting and repulsive picture the brush of his lifestyle paints—the late-night tears, the constant fear that grips abused children. Now picture God weeping for these children.

See your father's action ruining lives before your very eyes. Understand that if you continue this cycle, you will be Satan's tool, causing agonizing suffering in your children someday.

Step 2: *Fear God.* Many people have no idea what it means to fear God. It does not mean to be afraid of him, as if he were an angry, abusive parent. Nor does it mean you should hate him and run from him. Remember, God is not vengeful. He gave his Son, Jesus, so that we could have everlasting life.

*Fear* does mean to respect and reverence him. Yes, God punishes the wicked and sends people to hell if they say no to Jesus. But that is not out of meanness. He is just and cannot lie. He must keep his Word. "And to man He said, 'Behold, the fear of the Lord, that is wisdom; and to depart from evil is understanding'" (Job 28:28).

Step 3: *Decide against that kind of life.* Do more than make up your mind. Be accountable to someone. (It may be your counselor, a group of men who study God's Word with you, or someone wiser than you whom you totally trust.) Stay away from pornography, since it could lead you into your father's lifestyle. Satan will attack you in your weak areas, so identify them, and guard against attack there.

Please realize that while it is true that most abusers were abused themselves, it does not mean that all (or even most) abused children become abusers.

Be wise; stick close to help. Become a chooser and not a loser.

# 50
## Just Travelers

Life is a lot like golf. You have to go for the great shots, but at the same time you need to be ready to make more average or missed shots than perfect ones.

That's because we're human. Until we meet Jesus face-to-face, we have to come to grips with the fact that we love to sin and that our pride hinders our peace and happiness.

I'm a sinner, though I've been saved and am clear in God's sight. Just like anyone else, I still make mistakes and do wrong. I'm a dad who wants his kids to be perfect but still hangs on to his own secret sins and desires. I demand perfection of others, while I hide my own imperfections.

We Christians are travelers, not the travel agent, but it seems we seldom read the instructions God has given us to get where we're going. We pay about as much attention to them as I did to the directions when I built a new gas grill. After I had totally messed things up, I called my friend Kevin. He read the directions and had to start the project over. It only worked when we did it the right way.

Though God has given us the instructions, we seldom look at them until we're in trouble. When we do read them, sometimes we try to interpret his guidelines in ways God never planned us to. It's because we're sinners, and we want to do things our way.

One day my son decided I hated him because I had to spank him for lying. How little he knew of my love for him. If I didn't love him, I would take the easy way out and let him do whatever he wants without thinking of the consequences. Without love, I could never care enough to stick with being a dad day in and day out, watching, praying, and teaching him right from wrong.

Sometimes, when life gets tough, we Christians become like my son and decide that God doesn't love us anymore. Then our perceptions are clouded and we forget all the things he's done for us in the past. We blot out the fact that Jesus died for us, even when we wanted nothing to do with him.

I'm not excited about the fact that I sin. I don't enjoy having my pride knock me down spiritually. But I am relieved that I can stop trying to prove myself to the world and that I can start enjoying God and the life with which he has blessed me.

Know that you can let go of yourself. You don't need to be perfect or to make others that way. Live your best, one day at a time. When you sin, confess it and move back into God's fellowship. Instead of settling for yesterday's level of knowing God, strive for more. But don't set yourself an impossible standard of perfection.

> And we have come to know and have believed the love which God has for us. God is love, and the one who abides in love abides in God, and God abides in him. By this, love is perfected with us, that we may have confidence in the day of judgment; because as He is, so also are we in this world.
>
> 1 John 4:16–17

God is your perfection, which will only be complete when you join him in heaven.

Until then, you are a traveler, and life is a long journey (perhaps a megamarathon). It's not a sprint or a one-day event. Eliminate fears and worries from your mind by getting into God and his goodness.

Enjoy the trip. You know the final destination!